Iberian Ceramics: Muslim, Christian, Jewish Depictions

Ghufran 'Iffah Almasi

Abstract

For eight centuries, from 711 until 1492, a unique combination of political, cultural, and faith traditions coexisted in the mostly southern region of the Iberian Peninsula now called Spain. From the thirteenth century through the fifteenth century, two key production centers of luster glazed ceramics emerged in this region: Islamic-ruled Málaga and Christian-ruled Valencia. Muslim artisans using Islamic decorative motifs on reflective luster glaze ceramics created objects that patrons, including nobility and Christian royalty, clamored to collect. Initially, traditional Islamic decorative motifs dominated luster glazed ceramic production by Muslim artisans in Málaga; eventually, these artisans used combinations of Islamic and Christian motifs. As wars raged near Málaga, Muslim artisans migrated to Valencia—some converting to Christianity. Here, luster glazed ceramics evolved to include combinations of Islamic and Christian motifs, and, in one example, Islamic and Jewish motifs.

This investigation of Iberian luster glazed ceramics examines religious decorative motifs and their meaning by using a methodology that combines material culture studies and art history. Material culture studies seeks: (1) To find value and meaning in everyday objects; and (2) To introduce the understanding that visual motifs communicate in a different way than texts. Additions from art historians augment the conceptual framework: (1) Alois Riegl's concept of *Kunstwollen*—that every artistic expression and artifact that is produced is a distillation of the entirety of creator's worldview; and (2) Oleg Grabar's definition of Islamic art as one that overpowers and transforms ethnic or geographical traditions. In this dissertation, religious decorative elements on Iberian luster glazed ceramics are categorized as: (1) Floral and vegetative motifs; (2) Geometric symbols; (3) Figurative images; (4) Christian family coats of arms; and (5) Calligraphic inscriptions.

This dissertation will demonstrate how Muslim, Christian, and Jewish artisans used and combined the visual expressions of their respective faith traditions in motifs that appear on luster glazed ceramics created in the Iberian Peninsula under both Islamic and Christian ruled territories. Investigation of objects previously deemed not worthy of scholarly attention provides a more nuanced understanding of how religious co-existence (*convivencia* in Spanish) was negotiated in daily life.

Table of Contents

Abstract ii
Acknowledgments iv
Table of Contents v
List of Illustrations vi
Preface viii

Introduction 1
   The Context of Late-Medieval Iberia 1
      Shifting Geographies 3
      Religious and Ethnic Mixing in Medieval Iberia 7
      Lusterware Ceramics and their Religious Motifs 15
   Methodology 18
   Conclusions 27
   Chapter Overview 28

Chapter One 31
   The Development of Luster Glazed Ceramics 31
      Origins and Migration 31
      Techniques, Materials, and Designs 36
      The Islamic Context 40

Chapter Two 50
   Málaga's Emergence as an Economic, Artistic, and Cultural Center 50
      Alhambra Vases: Traditional Islamic Motifs 53
      Dishes: Combining Islamic and Christian Motifs? 74

Chapter Three 85
   Valencia's Emergence as an Economic, Artistic, and Cultural Center 85
      Replicating Traditional Islamic Motifs 92
      Christian Family Coats of Arms Motifs 104
      Islamic and Christian Motifs 118
      Islamic and Jewish Motifs 131

Chapter Four 138
   Conclusion 138

List of Illustrations

Table 1. *Timeline of Islamic Rule in Iberia 711-1492.* 5
Table 2. *Religious and Ethnic Mixing in Medieval Iberia.* 9
Table 3. *Timeline of Origins and Migration of Luster Glazed Ceramics.* 32
Table 4. *Luster Glazed Ceramics in Iberia: Malaga & Valencia* 143

Map 1. *The Spread of Islam: 622-750 C.E.* 1
Map 2. *Al-Andalus c. 900.* 4
Map 3. *Al-Andalus c. 1150.* 6
Map 4. *Al-Andalus c. 1300.* 7
Map 5. *Main Mediterranean and Black Sea Routes in Medieval Times c. 1092.* 34
Map 6. *Kingdoms of the Iberian Peninsula during the fourteenth and fifteenth centuries highlighting Málaga.* 51
Map 7. *Kingdoms of the Iberian Peninsula during the fourteenth and fifteenth centuries highlighting Valencia and environs.* 86

Figure 1. *Alhambra Vase (1)*, Probably Málaga, late thirteenth century, height: 128 cm. Galleria Regionale della Sicilia, Palermo. 58
Figure 2. *Alhambra Vase (1):* Detail 60
Figure 3. *Alhambra Vase (2).* Probably Málaga, early fourteenth century, height: 117 cm. State Hermitage Museum, St. Petersburg. 63
Figure 4. *Alhambra Vase (2):* Detail 67
Figure 5. *Alhambra Vase (3).* Probably Málaga, late fourteenth-early fifteenth century, height: 77.2 cm. Smithsonian Institution: Freer Gallery, Washington, D.C. 70
Figure 6. *Alhambra Vase (3):* Detail 71
Figure 7. *Bowl with a Horseman Spearing a Serpent.* Probably Málaga, late fourteenth or early fifteenth century, width: 44 cm, depth 7.6 cm. Metropolitan Museum, New York City 75
Figure 8. *Bowl with a Horseman Spearing a Serpent:* Detail 75
Figure 9. *Bowl.* Málaga, 1425-1450, width: 51.2 cm., height: 20.1 cm. Victoria and Albert Museum, London 80
Figure 10. *Bowl:* Detail 80
Figure 11. *The Last Supper,* by Jaume Ferrer the Elder or Pere Teixidor, early fifteenth century, tempera on wood, 107 x 36 cm. Originally from the church of Santa Constança in Linya; currently in Regional Diocesan Museum of Solsona, Solsona. 91
Figure 12. *The Last Supper:* Details 91
Figure 13. *Bowl with Fatima's Hand and Paradise Keys.* Possibly Manises or Paterna, fourteenth-fifteenth centuries, width: 12.5 cm, height: 7.3 cm. González Martí National Museum of Ceramic and Sumptuary Arts, Valencia. 94
Figure 14. *Lustreware Basin.* Manises, 1376 – 1425, width: 38 cm, height: 5.5 cm. González Martí National Museum of Ceramic and Sumptuary Arts, Valencia 98
Figure 15. *Deep Dish.* Probably Manises, c. 1430, width: 45.1 cm, height: 6 cm. The Cloisters Collection—Metropolitan Museum, New York City 100
Figure 16. *Plate.* Probably Manises, late fourteenth -early fifteenth centuries, width: 44.9 cm, height: 7 cm. The Cloisters Collection—Metropolitan Museum of Art, New York City 103
Figure 17. *Plate with the Arms of Blanche of Navarre.* Manises, 1427-38, width: 40 cm. The Cloisters Collection—Metropolitan Museum, New York City 106
Figure 18. *Deep Dish.* Manises, 1430-1460, width: 47.6 cm. The Cloisters Collection—Metropolitan Museum, New York City 109
Figure 19. *Dish.* Manises, 1430-70, width: 44.6 cm. Victoria and Albert Museum, London 112
Figure 20. *Plate.* Manises, 1470-1490, width: 43.2 cm. The Cloisters Collection—Metropolitan Museum, New York City 116
Figure 21. *Dish with Heraldic Shield.* Manises, 1470-1500, width: 43.5 cm. Metropolitan Museum, New York City 116
Figure 22. *Ewer Basin.* Valencia, c. 1525-1575, 37 cm. The Walters Art Museum, Baltimore 116

Figure 23. *Brasero Dish.* Manises, late fifteenth-early sixteenth centuries, width: 49.1 cm. Metropolitan Museum, New York City 116

Figure 24. *Plate.* Manises, 1430-1450, width: 37.3 cm. The Cloisters Collections—Metropolitan Museum, New York City 119

Figure 25. *Dish.* Probably Manises, c. 1450, width: 45.4 cm. The Cloisters Collection—Metropolitan Museum of Art, New York City 122

Figure 26. Comparison: (fig. 7) *Bowl with Horseman Spearing Serpent* & (fig. 25) *Dish* 124

Figure 27. *Plate.* Probably Manises, c. 1430-1460, width: 45.4 cm. The Cloister Collection—Metropolitan Museum, New York City 126

Figure 28. *Deep Dish.* Manises, c.1440, width: 47.2 cm. The Cloisters Collection—Metropolitan Museum, New York City 129

Figure 29. *Deep Dish:* Side view 129

Figure 30. *Seder Plate from Pre-Expulsion Spain.* Probably Valencia, c. 1480, width: 57 cm. The Israel Museum, Jerusalem..132

Introduction

The Context of Late-Medieval Iberia

In 711, Arab and North African Berber forces crossed the narrow Strait of Gibraltar and rapidly established Muslim control over most of the Iberian Peninsula according to Oleg Grabar, Islamic art historian.[1] This marked the furthest successful incursion into European territory by followers of Islam (see Map 1); it was less than a hundred years after the death of the Prophet Muhammad.[2] For nearly the next eight centuries, until 1492, multiple political and religious dynamics shaped a unique cultural mix in parts of the Iberian Peninsula now called Spain. By 756, one Muslim ruler united

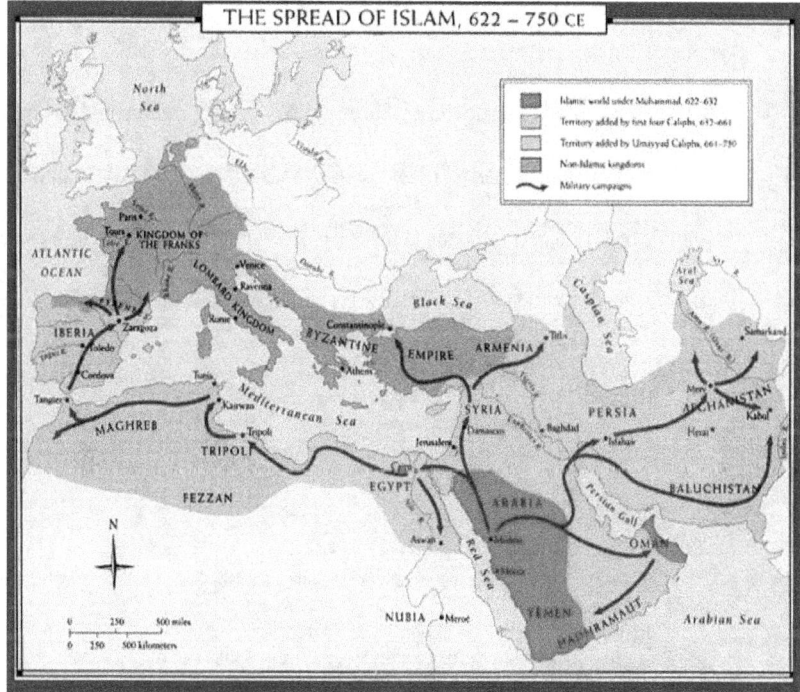

Map 1. *The Spread of Islam: 622-750 C.E.*

---

[1] Oleg Grabar, "Islamic Spain—The First Four Centuries: An Introduction," in *Al-Andalus: The Art of Islamic Spain,* ed. Jerrilynn Dodds. (New York: The Metropolitan Museum of Art, 1992), 3.

[2] The Prophet Muhammad died in 633. Islamic forces made campaigns into Constantinople and Central France that were not successful.

the region under his command. Prince 'Ab al Rahman I (the last surviving member of the Umayyad Dynasty of Damascus, Syria) had escaped the slaughter of his family[3] by fleeing to the west and arriving ultimately in Iberia. The Prince escaped through North Africa and gathered an army in Morocco aided by allegiances through his mother's Berber heritage.[4] With this army, due to weak governance in the southern Iberian region, Prince 'Ab al Rahman I conquered and ruled most of Iberia—now called *Al-Andalus* in Arabic.

In determining the etymology of *Al-Andalus*, the first word *'al'* is the Arabic definite article.[5] What *'al'* is defining, that is the *'Andalus'* moniker, is disputed and various. There are contradictory interpretations as well as contradictory understandings of the derivation of the name. The Arabic etymology of *Al-Andalus* could be one of three Arabic names meaning either: (1) "land of the Vandals;"[6] 2) "Island of Atlantis" or "The Atlantic;"[7] or (3) "to become green at the end of the summer."[8] The Spanish name *Andalucía* (spelled "Andalusia" in English) is clearly derivative of the Arabic *Al-Andalus*

---

[3] Those who committed the massacre brought about a change of rulers and the establishment of the Abassid Dynasty.
[4] "Berber" refers to pre-Arab inhabitants of North Africa. Grabar, "Islamic Spain," 6.
[5] "An article, as English *the,* that classes as identified or definite the noun it modifies." *Dictionary.com*, s.v. "definite article," accessed: February 19, 2016, http://dictionary.reference.com/browse/definite-article.
[6] "Vandals" refers to the Germanic Tribe which briefly colonized parts of Iberia in the early fifth century. Reinhart A. P. Dozy, *Recherches Sur L'Histoire Et la Littérature de L'Espagne Pendant Le Moyen Age*. (Charleston: BiblioLife, 2009), 303.
[7] Joaquín Vallvé , *La división territorial de la España musulmana*. (Madrid: Consejo Superior de Investigaciones Cientificas, Instituto de Filología—Departamento de Estudios Arabes, 1986), 55–59.
[8] Maryam Noor Beig, "Andalusia When It Was...," HispanicMuslims.com, accessed: February 19, 2016, http://www.hispanicmuslims.com/andalusia/andalusia.html

and originated in the thirteenth century to refer to the geographical region under Islamic rule at the time.[9]

Another important distinction covers the usage of Islam versus Muslim as the two are often used interchangeably and erroneously in Western contexts. Islam (*'islām*) in Arabic means "submission" from *'aslama* meaning "submit (to God)." Islam refers to the faith of the Muslims: "the monotheistic faith regarded as revealed through Muhammad as the Prophet of Allah."[10] The adherents of the Islamic faith are known as Muslims. For example, in this dissertation the phrase Islamic rule refers to the religious governance structures in al-Andalus while those who rule are the Muslim rulers.

Prince 'Ab al Rahman I, the last member of the Syrian Umayyad Dynasty, was the first Muslim ruler to unify more than two thirds of the territories on the Iberian Peninsula (see Map 2). 'Ab al Rahman I established a dynasty named the 'Emirate of Córdoba'—so named because *Emir* is a title of many Muslim rulers and because Córdoba served as the Emirate's capital city.[11]

Shifting Geographies

The geographic reach of Prince 'Ab al Rahman I's rule (see Map 2) extended well over two thirds of the Iberian Peninsula. Dodds and Walker describe this al-Andalus as "an elegant capital for both the east and west."[12]

---

[9] Manuel González Jiménez, *Andalucía a Debate y Otros Estudios* (Seville: University of Seville, 1998), 16–17. '*Andalucía*' continues to be the Spanish appellation used to describe the southern Iberian Peninsula today.

[10] *Oxford Dictionaries.com*, s.v. "Islam," accessed August 06, 2016 http://www.oxforddictionaries.com/us/definition/american_english/islam.

[11] *Oxford Dictionaries.com*, s.v. "Emir," accessed August 08, 2016 http://www.oxforddictionaries.com/us/definition/american_english/emir.

[12] Jerrilynn Dodds and Daniel Walker, "Introduction," in *Al-Andalus: The Art of Islamic Spain*, ed. Jerrilynn Dodds. (New York: The Metropolitan Museum of Art, 1992), xix.

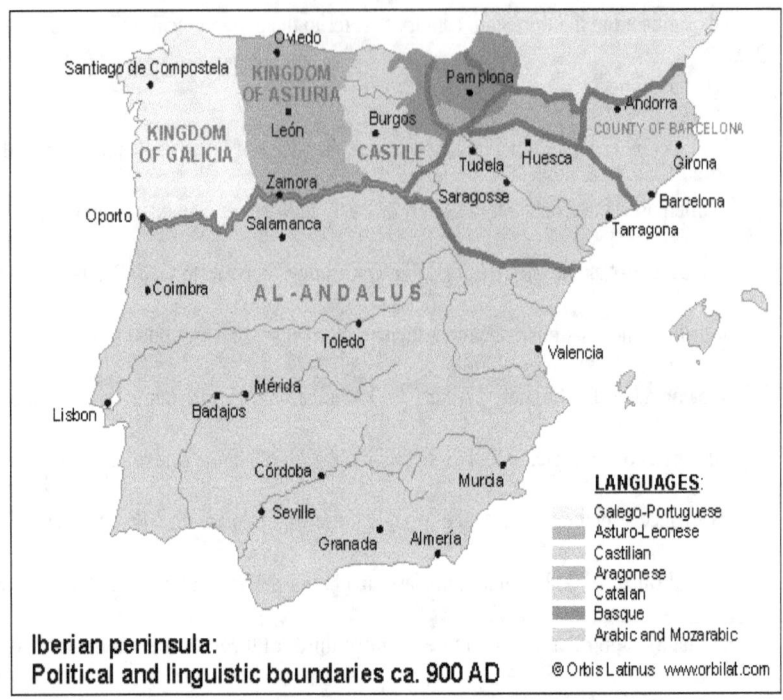

Map 2. *Al-Andalus c. 900.*

In 929 'Abd al-Rahman III, a direct descendant of Prince 'Ab al Rahman I, proclaimed himself *Caliph* which means the ruler regarded as a successor to Muhammad.[13] His descendants continued the lineage of this Iberian Umayyad Caliphate ruling into the eleventh century.

In 1031, the Umayyad Caliphate broke up into principalities called *taifas* or *Taifa Kingdoms*. Maria Rosa Menocal, Scholar of Medieval Culture and History, explains that "[i]n Arabic *taifa* means 'party' or 'faction.' And in this case it means a splinter party, a breakaway from the mainstream."[14] Skirmishes, strife, and relentless incursions from

---

[13] *OxfordDictionaries.com*, s.v. "Caliph," accessed August 08, 2016, http://www.oxforddictionaries.com/us/definition/american_english/caliph.

[14] Maria Rosa Menocal, *The Ornament of the World: How Muslims, Jews and Christians Created a Culture of Tolerance in Medieval Spain* (Boston: Little Brown, 2002), 39.

Timeline of Islamic Rule in Iberia 711 to 1492				
Umayyad Emirate & Caliphate	Taifa Kingdoms	Almoravid Dynasty	Almohad Dynasty	Nasrid Dynasty
756-1031	1031-1086	1090-1145	1145-1232	1232-1492

Table 1. *Timeline of Islamic Rule in Iberia 711-1492.*

northern Christian rulers marked the next several decades during which time the Muslim rulers of the *Taifa* Kingdoms (1031-1086) appealed to a series of Moroccan Berber forces to repel the *'Reconquista'*[15] (or 're- conquering') Christian forces. These included the Almoravid Dynasty (1090-1145) and Almohad Dynasty (1145-1232) with varying degrees of success.[16] (See Map 3.) *Taifa* Kings were unable to maintain control once the armed forces landed in Iberia. As Buresi and El Aallaoui explain, the twelfth century Moroccan Berber Almohad Dynasty was extremely powerful not only throughout Morocco but that "Al-Andalus followed the fate of North Africa and all Islamic Iberia was under Almohad rule by 1172."[17] Even with these powerful interventions, Islamic ruled land in Iberia continued to diminish.

By 1232, the Nasr' family emerged to rule as the Nasrid Dynasty, the last of the Islamic Dynasties to rule in the now much reduced region of Iberia, also known as the

---

[15] "Reconquest" is a problematic term as Menocal elucidates: "One of the many problems with 'reconquest' is the suggestion that it means ideologically pure and politically uncompromising stances between Christiana nd Muslim in this land, and yet even at the most basic diplomatic and military levels, one sees... that political alliances in practice often overrode the supposed ideological dividing lives." María Rosa Menocal, "Visions of Al-Andalus," in *The Literature of Al-Andalus*, ed. María Rosa Menocal et al. (Cambridge: Cambridge University Press, 2000), 5.

[16] "Heilbrunn Timeline of Art History Iberian Peninsula, 1000–1400 A.D.," Metropolitan Museum, accessed August 08, 2016, http://www.metmuseum.org/toah/ht/07/eusi.html.

[17] Pascal Buresi and Hicham El Aallaoui. *Governing the Empire: Provincial Administration in the Almohad Caliphate 1224-1269* (Leiden: Brill, 2012), 3.

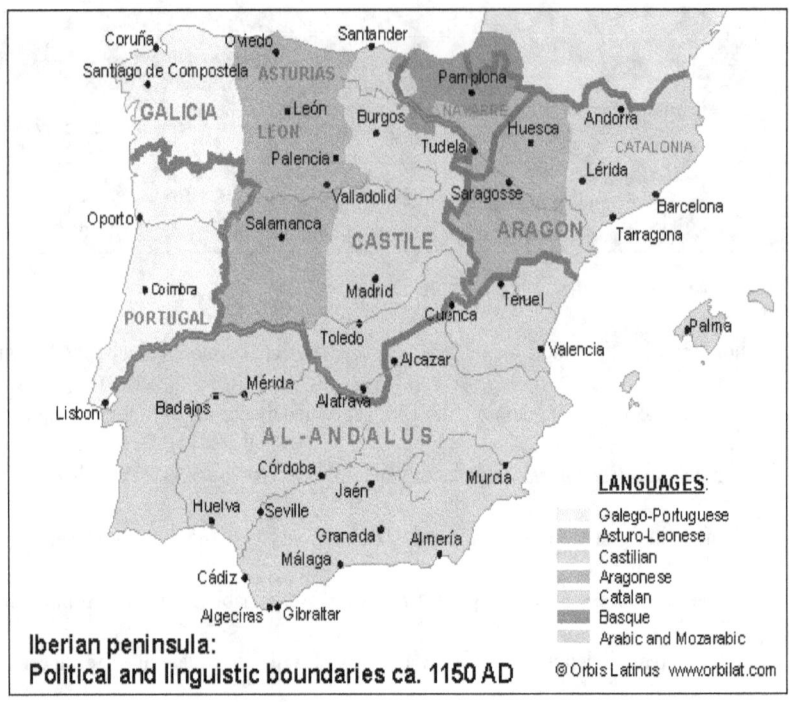

Map 3. *Al-Andalus c. 1150.*

Kingdom of Granada. In contrast to the previous map, Map 4 shows that by the fourteenth century the geographic and political boundaries that defined parameters for interactions of Muslims, Christians, and Jews in the Iberian Peninsula had changed dramatically. The establishment of the Nasrid Dynasty was done in the context of "the wolves howling mightily at the door" according to Menocal.[18] Specifically, she notes that the Alhambra Palace built by Nasrid rulers in their capital, Granada, serves to "monumentalize the inevitability of loss."[19] In 1492, the Nasrid Dynasty and the Islamic era of dominance in *Al-Andalus,* ended with Christian rulers Queen Isabella of Castile

---

[18] Menocal, "Visions," 5.
[19] Menocal, "Visions," 7.

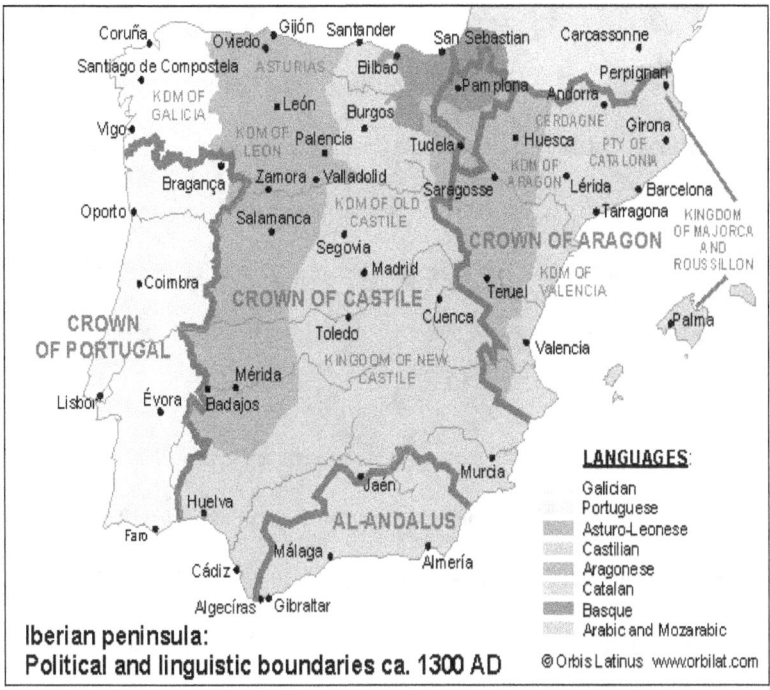

Map 4. *Al-Andalus c. 1300.*

and King Ferdinand of Aragon marching "up the hill to the Alhambra to take formal possession of Granada dressed in their Arab finery."[20]

Religious and Ethnic Mixing in Medieval Iberia

Three names can be used to describe the Medieval Iberian Peninsula: in Arabic *Al- Andalus*, in Spanish *Hispania*, and in Hebrew *Sepharad*.[21] Each of these names, used simultaneously by their respective Muslim, Christian, and Jewish populations, reveals the complex mix of cultural and religious identities. Menocal cautions "much of the nomenclature we must employ…is imprecise or controversial, or simply reveals the

---

[20] Menocal, *Ornament of the World*, 270.
[21] Czerny Brasuell, Mishael Caspi, and Baltazar Fra-Molinero, "Medieval Spain: Muslims, Jews, and Christians," *Bates College Courses* (2015-2016), accessed February 7, 2016, http://abacus.bates.edu/~bframoli/medieval/descripcion.html

vexed nature" of describing the geographical area itself;[22] it depends upon who was doing the naming. Categorizing the population based on faith traditions requires a nuanced understanding of how people identified themselves. For the historical scope of this paper—that is, pre-modern faith communities in the fourteenth and fifteenth centuries—faith identity was understood to be a corporate or group identity, e.g., a community of faith versus the modern understanding of individuals engaging with their own faith.

While faith is a useful category for distinguishing between members of the population in Iberia, there is more historical evidence of the beliefs of the small number of rulers as opposed to the beliefs of the many inhabitants. Evidence of diversity of beliefs held within and among faith traditions exists in the form of edicts proscribing behavior as well as in persecution and wars. Thus the labels dividing the population into separate faith traditions refers more to the beliefs of those with the most power than the populace as a whole. It is precisely this concern that inspires recent scholarship examining objects of daily life to create a more nuanced understanding of historical contexts in Medieval Iberia.

The Muslim population arriving on the Iberian Peninsula in the eighth century "were Arabs from the east and Berbers from North Africa, the majority of whom were totally arabicized" according to Oleg Grabar, citing sources from Muslim geographers. Status for these Muslims increased particularly if they "could claim descent from immigrants from the east" (or Arabia) and the birthplace of the Prophet Muhammad,

---

[22] "*Hispania* (the name inherited from antiquity) meant for Christians, all of the peninsula, and included the Muslim-occupied lands; while for the Arab historians its equivalent, *Ishbaniya*, was usually applied only to Christian Spain. *Al Andalus*, for the Arabs, similarly could encompass either the whole peninsula or only the portion under Muslim rule." Menocal, "Visions," 5.

\multicolumn{2}{c}{**Religious and Ethnic Mixing in Medieval Iberia**}
Name	*Definition*
Converso	Convert most frequently used for Jews who converted to Christianity; can mean anyone who converts
Morisco	'Moors' who converted to Christianity
Mozarab	Christians who adopted Muslim customs such as types of clothing and food as well as speaking Arabic
Múdejar	Muslims who converted to Christianity
Muwalladūn	Christian natives of Spain whose ancestors converted to Islam

Table 2. *Religious and Ethnic Mixing in Medieval Iberia.*

considered themselves the social elite."[23] This reverence and social stature afforded to those originating from the east is personified in the first ruler to unite the Islamic forces in Iberia: Prince 'Ab al Rahman I, the last member of the Umayyad dynasty, who hailed from Syria. The Muslim conquerors did not remain entirely separate from the local population as Grabar explains: "[T]he immigrants married indigenous women, since there are almost no records of Arab or Berber women who came to the peninsula." These marriages created a mixed culture from the beginning of Islamic rule in Iberia, "the nature of which probably contributed much to the unique character of the Arab Muslim civilization that developed in al-Andalus."[24] By the fourteenth century, some Muslim adherents had converted to Christianity and became known as *Múdejar* (see **Table 2. Religious and Ethnic Mixing in Medieval Iberia**).

The Christian population on the Iberian Peninsula reflected a combination of cultural influences as well. From 206 B.C.E. Romans ruled over an already diverse

---

[23] Grabar, "Islamic Spain," 6.
[24] Grabar, "Islamic Spain," 4.

population in Iberia. Nancy Gratton explains, "By the time of the Roman conquest, Andalusia was the home of great ethnic diversity, being comprised of Africans, Jews, Phoenicians, and Greeks, as well as descendants of the indigenous Celtiberian peoples."[25] In the fifth century, Visigoths, a combination of Germanic tribes from northern Europe, entered Iberia initially as allies of Roman forces. However, these Visigoths not only helped to conquer the indigenous people, they took over the Roman forces as well and ruled for over three embattled centuries. By the early eighth century, Christians in Iberia were buffeted by conflict amongst the Visigoth rulers. Though Visigoth kings converted to Catholicism in the late 6th century, early Iberian Visigoths adhered initially to pagan beliefs and then later to Arian Christian beliefs claiming the unity of God.[26] Grabar describes the population as having been "recently divided" by different interpretations of Christian doctrine, from the Arian concept of unity to the Catholic concept of trinity. In addition, there "was a vacuum of centralized power with irreducible internal conflicts. Its political leadership was weak, its population scattered over a huge territory and torn by competing concerns, both ethnic and spiritual, that were at large in a vast land."[27]

With the initial arrival of conquering Muslims, Christians did not convert very rapidly to the new Islamic faith, according to Grabar.[28] However, with time, he explains, a "large number of Spanish Muslims" became known as *muwalladūn*: "Christian natives of Spain...[who] converted to Islam out of religious conviction or to gain higher social

---

[25] Nancy Gratton, "Andalusians," in *Encyclopedia of World Cultures*, 1996, accessed February 19, 2016, http://www.encyclopedia.com/doc/1G2-3458000614.html
[26] Arian Christianity asserts that "Jesus is the Son of God, he was created by God at a point in time, is distinct from God, and is therefore subordinate to God. Arian teachings were first attributed to Arius, a Christian preacher in Alexandria, Egypt in the late third and early fourth centuries." Charles William Previté-Orton, *The Shorter Cambridge Medieval History* (Cambridge: Cambridge University Press, 1979), 145.
[27] Grabar, "Islamic Spain," 4.
[28] Grabar, "Islamic Spain," 4.

status or economic advantages."[29] While the Christian population on the Iberian Peninsula was technically subject to the regulation of the hierarchy in Rome, Catholic leaders during this period were, as Grabar defines, "admittedly remote and inaccessible and often at odds with local theological, liturgical, and social aspirations." Christians who adhered closely to their faith tradition but who acquired aspects of Arab culture from the Muslim community were called *Mozarabs*.[30] Grabar states that *Mozarab* Christians "held diverse religious views and had mixed feelings about their past as well as about the contemporary scene, created an extremely original culture...often very close to the Arab culture of Muslims or to the Muslim culture of Arabs."[31] Menocal notes that some *Mozarabs* were so "Arabized" that they "had to have their Bibles translated into Arabic."[32]

By the early eighth century, the Jewish population of Iberia had endured over a century of persecution under Visigoth Kings who had converted to Catholicism in the late sixth century. Solomon Katz states that, under the rule of Catholic Visigoth rulers, Jews faced increasing and pervasive persecution. Further, he suggests that there may have been a "degree of complicity which the Jews had in the Islamic invasion of 711." Katz notes that, "In 694 Jews were accused of conspiring with the Muslims across the Mediterranean. Declared traitors, the Jews, including baptized ones, found their property confiscated and themselves enslaved."[33] Throughout these times of persecution, many Jews converted to Christianity and became known as *converso*s, or 'converted ones.'

---

[29] Grabar, "Islamic Spain," 6.
[30] Grabar, "Islamic Spain," 6.
[31] Grabar, "Islamic Spain," 6.
[32] Menocal, "Visions," 13.
[33] Solomon Katz, *The Jews in the Visigothic and Frankish Kingdoms of Spain and Gaul* (Cambridge, Massachusetts: The Mediaeval Society of America, 1937), 21.

The earliest reference to Jews in Spain, according to Philip Schaff, is in a Christian Council of Elvira's decree from the early fourth century which addresses "proper Christian behavior with regard to the Jews of Spain, notably forbidding marriage between Jews and Christians."[34] In contrast, evidence of Jews flourishing under Islamic rule in al-Andalus abounds. Grabar describes their particularly important role: "they were among the richest and most successful merchants from Spain."[35] While many Sephardic Jews attained financial success, academic accomplishment, and were valued, for the most part, under Islamic rule within Iberia, in matters of faith they maintained strong ties to other regions. Grabar notes that Iberian Jews "consulted the rabbis and learned men of Iraq in matters of faith. Moreover, they were connected through marriage with their coreligionists in North Africa, Sicily, Egypt, and even India."[36]

The balance of power between these faith traditions was "maintained a workable equilibrium" by the Islamic rulers, states Grabar.[37] While the governing power was Islamic, the populace included significant numbers of Christians and Jews. Islamic law included the *dhimma*—an ordinance that allowed for Christians and Jews to practice their own traditions within certain restrictions.[38] Christians and Jews were required to pay an annual tax as well as acknowledge the ultimate authority of Islam.

Menocal acknowledges the challenges of categorizing this era of religious, ethnic and cultural mixing in Islamic Iberia. She notes that previous generations of scholars

---

[34] Philip Schaff, "§55. The Councils of Elvira, Arles, and Ancyra," *History of the Christian Church, Volume II: Ante-Nicene Christianity. A.D. 100-325* (Grand Rapids, Michigan: Calvin College Christian Classics Ethereal Library, 2005), accessed February 5, 2016, http://www.ccel.org/ccel/schaff/hcc2.html.
[35] Grabar, "Islamic Spain," 6-7.
[36] Grabar, "Islamic Spain," 6-7.
[37] Grabar, "Islamic Spain," 6-7.
[38] Prince 'Ab al Rahman I "brought the concept of *dhimma* from Syria. The Umayyad Dynasty ruled over a population in Damascus that was predominantly Christians and Jews." Menocal, "Ornament," 38.

seem to have "overlooked" over seven hundred years of history as it did not fit neatly into understandings of Western or European history.[39] Menocal emphasizes the complex and unique culture created in Islamic Iberia of *convivencia* which translates from Spanish to 'coexistence' or 'living together.' *Convivencia,* as defined by Menocal, is "one of those much contested and vexed terms" which is "only problematic if we insist on some sort of uniformity and neatness;" the term has "come to imply certain level of cultural comingling that most people assume must be based on a certain level of religious tolerance."[40]

Many artifacts from this time, according to Menocal, combine imagery from divergent traditions (such as a church decorated with horseshoe arches and Arabic writing) emerge precisely because of the concept of *convivencia* and also because of the simultaneous ethos of *reconquista*. These artifacts combined imagery of different faiths, states Menocal, "precisely because *convivencia* and *reconquista* could and did exist side by side, at the same time, in the same place. The conceptual error that has plagued all sides of the study of what some call Medieval Spain, and others al-Andalus, and yet others Sefarad…is the assumption that these phenomena, reconquest and convivencia, are thoroughgoing and thus mutually exclusive."[41]

Historian Melquiades Andres Martin acknowledges the underlying tensions of maintaining a secular coexistence between faith communities with divergent beliefs as he states, "Convivencia secular, muchas veces difícil, a veces hosca y de guerra

---

[39] Menocal, "Visions," 14.
[40] Menocal, "Visions," 14.
[41] Menocal, "Visions," 14.

declarada."[42] Brasuell, et al, educators at Bates College, underscore the potential and actual violence in late medieval Iberia thus: "[t]he term *convivencia* has been gaining currency to express the historical circumstance of Medieval Spain and the existence within it of three official religions, three cultures, and three literary traditions. Yet the history of Medieval Spain was violent."[43]

While not downplaying the mixing of cultures and imagery from Muslim, Christian, Jewish in architecture and artifacts, Grabar too has countered a simplistic interpretation of the '*convivencia*' with what he deems is perhaps a more realistic understanding. Grabar states that the first four centuries of Islamic dominance of *Al-Andalus* were not without conflict but that disagreements tended to be able to be resolved without full scale clashes, especially in the southern region that did not share a border with the Christian north.[44] This dynamic changed: and the final four centuries saw more full scale battles occurring region by region between Islamic forces in the south and Catholic forces in the north pushing their agenda of re-conquering the land ceded to Islamic rule.

Art historians Jerrilynn Dodds and Vivian Mann, along with historian Thomas Glick note that recently scholars have been questioning past theoretical constructs which have either presumed one of two assumptions: (1) That the cultures within Andalusia remained somehow discreet entities unto themselves, purely Islamic, Christian, or Jewish with little interaction; or (2) That though there was a mix of faith traditions in the region, that they were essentially subsumed in the over-arching Muslim aesthetic and cultural

---

[42] "Secular coexistence [was]often difficult, sometimes hostile and even an outright war." Melquiades Andrés Martín, *Ensayo sobre el cristianismo español* (Madrid: Biblioteca de Autores Cristianos, 2005), 33.
[43] Czerny Brasuell, et al, "Medieval Spain," Course Description.
[44] Grabar, "Islamic Spain," 4.

influences.[45] Recent scholarship has sought a more nuanced understanding of multicultural interactions as evidenced by the creation of decorative objects as ceramic ware—whether it was for daily use or for courtly use—that reveals a cross section of inspiration and imagery from multiple faith traditions.

This dissertation will demonstrate how Muslim, Christian, and Jewish artisans used and combined the visual expressions of their respective faith traditions in motifs that appear on luster glazed ceramics created in the Iberian Peninsula under both Islamic and Christian ruled territories. Investigation of objects previously deemed not worthy of scholarly attention provides a more nuanced understanding of how religious *convivencia* was negotiated in daily life.

Lusterware Ceramics and their Religious Motifs

In the thirteenth century, when Muslim artisans fled political upheavals in Egypt and Persia immigrating in great numbers to a more politically stable *Al Andalus*, they brought significant contributions to the arts of the Iberian Peninsula. Included among the artisans were ceramicists who brought with them traditional Islamic decorative motifs and advanced metallic glazing and firing techniques enabling the creation of a new style of pottery in Iberia. In particular, Muslim artisans brought carefully guarded recipes for ceramic glazes using copper and silver granules that, when painted on ceramic ware and fired at high temperatures in a kiln, created a radiant, reflective lustrous surface. The beauty of the luster glaze combined with Islamic symbols on the ceramic ware captured the attention not only of Muslim patrons but also of Christian patrons in the region (and beyond), such that Christians intent on re-conquering the land under Islamic rule were at

---

[45] Jerrilynn D. Dodds, Vivian B. Mann and Thomas F. Glick, ed., *Convivencia: Jews, Muslims, and Christians in Medieval Spain* (New York: Jewish Museum, 1992), 113.

the same time commissioning exquisite luster glazed ceramic ware to fill their homes. These ceramic objects are referred to by many names including *loza dorada*,[46] lusterware, and Hispano-Moresque Pottery. For the purposes of this dissertation they will be referred to as luster glazed ceramics.

In southern Iberia, the last bastion of *Al-Andalus*, the Kingdom of Granada, the 'special kind of pottery'[47] that emerged was distinctive for its dazzling reflective luster glaze. Among a wide variety of styles of these ceramic works, a subset of luster glazed ceramics contained multiple Islamic, Christian, and Jewish religious symbols and inscriptions.

The most prolific production center of luster glazed ceramics emerged first in Islamic-ruled Málaga. However, due to ongoing religious wars between Muslims and Christians in Málaga, there was a dramatic decline in the number of Muslim artisans and thus a decline in the quantity of luster glazed ceramics produced there. In contrast, in Christian-ruled Valencia, religious wars between Christians and Muslims had subsided. Simultaneously, while conflict was increasing in Malaga it had decreased in Valencia. Therefore Valencia overtook and surpassed Málaga in production of luster glazed ceramics by both Muslim and Christian artisans. The luster glazed ceramics reflect not only the brilliance and craftsmanship of the artisans who created them, but the decorative schemes also reflect the mix of their Muslim, Christian, and Jewish values and faith traditions.

There is a significant body of fourteenth and fifteenth century Iberian luster glazed ceramic ware with religious motifs preserved in collections and museums to allow

---

[46] *"Loza Dorada"* translates from Spanish to English as "Golden Glazed Ceramics."
[47] Guillermo Rosselló Bordoy, "The Ceramics of Al-Andalus," in *Al-Andalus: The Art of Islamic Spain,* ed. Jerrilynn Dodds. (New York: The Metropolitan Museum of Art, 1992), 101.

for comparison and analysis of aesthetic, functional, and ritual use. The subset of luster glazed ceramic bowls, plates, and platters to be investigated in the following chapters are those which contain Muslim, Christian, or Jewish imagery—and often a combination of religious inscriptions.

The luster glazed ceramic ware with combinations of imagery from different faiths can be categorized as utilizing the following: (1) Floral and vegetative motifs; (2) Geometric symbols; (3) Calligraphic inscriptions in Arabic, Latin and Hebrew; (4) Figurative images; and (5) Family coats of arms. Of these categories, the most numerous examples now in existence are the Christian family coat of arms ceramic platters. There are several surviving ceramic platters with Christian calligraphy inscribed in Latin, but many fewer of these ceramic wares are those that combine figurative imagery with both Muslim and Christian references. The rarest example found in the one platter with both Jewish calligraphy surrounded by Muslim patterns.

It is important to view these objects as works with their own aesthetic integrity—as complete works unto themselves. Hoffman describes handcrafted objects—such as luster glazed ceramics decorated with combined religious motifs—as providing "a neutral territory" for encountering visual representations of stories common to several faith traditions where users could "partake of a fluid and interchangeable vocabulary."[48] According to Hoffman, local culture and identity shaped these objects more than theology or ideology: the "visual vocabulary was never intended to be segregated" into categories based upon faith traditions. "The polarization between Christian and Islamic

---

[48] Eva R. Hoffman, "Christian-Islamic Encounters on Thirteenth-Century Ayyubid Metalwork: Local Culture, Authenticity, and Memory." *Gesta* 43, no. 2 (2004): 131.

themes is the result of conditioning by later historians rather than by…artists, patrons and viewers."[49]

Methodology

This dissertation utilizes the methodology of material culture studies as it has been incorporated into the field of art history to examine the hybrid religious motifs on luster glazed ceramics from the Late Medieval Iberian Peninsula. Investigating motifs that combine Muslim, Christian, and Jewish imagery and styles on luster ware ceramic objects requires an approach that values study of objects which have not been considered worthy of scholarly attention. Only recently have art historians systematically integrated material culture studies as a part of their discipline. Therefore, it is important to understand the historical constructs of how these two formerly separate methodologies have fused.

Material Culture Studies

Material culture is a phrase originating in disciplines of archaeology, sociology, and anthropology as a way of describing and examining what remains of a culture and what we can deduce about that lived experience and culture from its surviving artifacts. Material culture has had multiple meanings. According to historian of art education Paul E. Bolin and arts educator Doug Blandy, the term material culture has been used two ways: "First, it is utilized to capture the entire breadth of human made or modified objects, forms, and expressions; and second, it…describes a "method of cultural inquiry employing physical objects as primary data." Addressing this ambiguity and clarifying the distinction of terminology, scholars "now employ the separate terms 'material culture' and 'material culture studies' to describe features of their work. 'Material

---

[49] Hoffman, "Christian-Islamic Encounters," 131.

culture' is used to reference artifacts, and other human-made forms…while 'material culture studies' is utilized to describe the effort undertaken to investigate and interpret the various forms, objects, and expression of material culture."[50]

Art historian Michael Yonan has taken on the task of articulating how material culture studies and art history have become fused; he explains the interdisciplinary appeal of using 'material culture studies' as a methodology: "material culture began as an attempt to extract information from objects left by prehistoric and nonliterate cultures. Lacking textual records from such societies, scholars turned to their material artifacts—bowls, architectural remains, religious objects, tools—to reconstruct long-lost or otherwise inaccessible ways of life."[51] Material culture has thus had as an equalizing effect—in justifying the study of a culture's everyday objects as well as its most precious objects. Yonan describes the methodological "result is a true 'transdiscipline' in which a great diversity of objects, paired with a wide selection of interpretive modes, results in seemingly limitless potential for understanding things and what they might mean or have meant for different communities and individuals in specific settings."[52]

Material culture studies has established the following criteria: (1) To find value and meaning in everyday objects; and (2) To introduce the concept of visual literacy into common understanding. Visual literacy means understanding that symbols and visual motifs communicate in a different way than texts—especially in contexts of limited literacy. Historians of archeology Dan Hicks and Mary C. Beaudry posit the need to

---

[50] Paul E. Bolin and Doug Blandy, "Beyond Visual Culture: Seven Statements of Support for Material Culture Studies in Art Education," *Studies in Art Education* 44, 3 (2003): 250-251.
[51] Michael Yonan, "Toward a Fusion of Art History and Material Culture Studies," *West 86th: A Journal of Decorative Arts, Design History, and Material Culture* 18, 2 (2011): 232, accessed December 28, 2015, http://www.west86th.bgc.bard.edu/articles/yonan.html.
[52] Yonan, "Toward a Fusion," 232.

examine the objects of material culture to gain a more accurate understanding of historical contexts.[53]

Art historian Thomas F. Mathews suggests that academic under-valuation of images in religious contexts taints our ability to comprehend the lived experience of followers of faith traditions in centuries past. Ironically he claims that even art historians "have been slow to address the power of images." He notes "[w]e are more accustomed to narrating events" in terms of "describing the winning images as a consequence of the political fortunes of one or another party." Instead, he claims, we need to imagine the possibility that it was the power of religious images rather than religious writings which "determined the outcome" of key power struggles. To do otherwise is to "imagine that art is chiefly decoration and illustration, that it merely echoes decisions made in a higher court of activity without taking part in the events of world history."[54]

Material culture studies has evolved from fields such as anthropology which, while studying non-westerners' material culture, gave preference to Western styles and objects. As Sociologist and Cultural Researcher Ian Woodward notes, "[a]ll too often it was a way of putting material culture into categories in such a way that marginalized and hierarchized the cultures that they came out of."[55] In going to a museum, material culture artifacts were used to show the supposed evolution of society: moving from 'simple' objects of non-westerners to 'advanced' objects of Europeans. It was a way of showing that Europeans were at the end of the evolution of society, while non-westerners were at the beginning.

---

[53] Dan Hicks and Mary C. Beaudry, ed., *The Oxford Handbook of Material Culture Studies* (Oxford: Oxford University Press, 2010), 5.
[54] Thomas F. Mathews, *The Clash of the Gods: A Reinterpretation of Early Christian Art* (Princeton: Princeton University Press, 1993), 4-5.
[55] Woodward, Ian, *Understanding Material Culture* (London: Sage Publications Ltd., 2007), 17.

Art History

Within art history, a discipline which began in eighteenth century Europe, there are antecedents to contemporary understandings of material culture studies. Michael Yonan asserts that valuation of object-based study has been implicit within art history from its origin but that "art history has tricked itself into believing that it is a discipline of images, when really it has always been a discipline of objects. Some of these objects are bearers of images, some are harder to understand as such, but all are objects nonetheless. More crucially, that object status insistently inflects and determines a work of art's potential meanings, a fact that the best art history has always recognized."[56]

This dissertation relies upon values and distinctions within traditional Western art history as developed by Alois Riegl (1858-1905). Riegl devoted keen attention to decorative arts and as a result introduced the notion of *Kunstwollen*. This German phrase is difficult to translate simply. *Kunstwollen* is a concept that conveys the relationship between an artistic expression and an artifact as the product of active engagement and interpretation of the individual and his/her world.[57] Thus, every artistic expression and artifact that is produced is a distillation of the entirety of creator's worldview. Art historian Jas' Elsner notes that the key tension in Riegl's approach is a tension of which Riegl himself was acutely aware. Elsner describes Riegl's concept of *Kunstwollen* as a

---

[56] Yonan, "Toward a Fusion," 240.
[57] This term "appears for the first time in *Spätrömische Kunstindustrie* (1901), a book that examines late antique art in the Roman period. Another key work by Riegl is *Stilfragen: Grundlegungen zu einer Geschichte der Ornamentik* (1893), a book on the historical continuity of art, in particular, ornamental art from the ancient Near East, Byzantium and Islam." Jas' Elsner, "From Empirical Evidence to the Big Picture: Some Reflections on Riegl's Concept of *Kunstwollen*," *Critical Inquiry* 32, no.4 (2006): 743.

"sense of being pulled in both directions—towards the satisfyingly described single object and at the same time the fully elaborated historical picture."[58]

Another concept Riegl articulated relates to value judgments on different kinds of art works. Art historian Otto Pächt summarizes Riegl's contribution in his book entitled *Stilfragen*, which translates to 'stylistic questions,' stating, here "for the first time the minor arts were treated as a major theme of history…Riegl's objective was to refute or minimize the influence of all external factors so that stylistic changes could be explained in terms of an internal or organic evolution, as a relatively autonomous development."[59] Riegl's notions of *Kunstwollen* and *Stilfragen* provide the conceptual basis for the discipline of art historical material culture studies that focus on heretofore unappreciated objects and imagery.

Yonan credits Riegl with a re-evaluation of assumptions with art history. He asserts, "[r]ecategorizing art history so that it is *not* focused around the image might seem like a misstep, but art-historical thinking has been flirting with this possibility for at least a century. Alois Riegl envisioned it when he distinguished purely optical qualities in art from haptic ones, and thereby defined artistic processes as existing along a continuum between seeing and touching."[60] Art historian Jules David Prown in 1982 redresses Riegl's desire to see objects become primary components of art-historical analysis. Yonan summarizes Prown's links between diverse objects as "their ability to reveal aspects of past cultures, not textually, but through the inherent and attached values assigned to them at different moments in their histories. These values reveal a great deal

---

[58] Elsner, "Riegl's Concept of *Kunstwollen*," 744.

[59] Otto Pächt, "Art Historians and Art Critics - vi: Alois Riegl," *The Burlington Magazine* 105, 722 (1963): 189.

[60] Haptic comes from the Greek *haptikos* and means "of or relating to the sense of touch." Yonan, "Toward a Fusion," 240.

about the past, and may do so in ways that other evidence does not disclose. Prown's methodology is therefore fundamentally historical in that he sees material culture studies as a tool for accessing lost cultural meanings."[61]

Implicit values of worth and judgment within Western art history has created separate and opposing categories of highly valued "fine arts" versus less worthy "decorative crafts." Explicit in the formulation of "high" and "low" art is what Yonan terms "an ancient yet persistent distinction between art, appreciated for purely aesthetic and principally visual qualities, and objects, which may possess aesthetic appeal but which also carry some more mundane, functional significance…Indeed, much recent art-historical inquiry has sought to undermine or muddle the distinction between 'high' and 'low' art, rendering the art-craft divide weaker today than at any point in the past century."[62]

Foundational scholars in art history "persistently privileged the visual aspects of art over the material." Yonan specifies: "Heinrich Wölfflin's formalism stressed the comparative method as a means of exploring artistic style, but the actual materiality of the paintings so analyzed is only a minor part of his equation. Erwin Panofsky's iconographical method, at least as promulgated in his popular essays published in the 1950s, likewise makes no strong demand on the interpreter to explore medium as a constituent of meaning…This has had the result of privileging the idea or image over the object as a thing, and much art-historical writing continues to undervalue materiality as a component of its scholarly mission."[63] Recognizing a long history of imbalanced scholarship in Western art history, Cynthia Robinson argues for reconsideration of the

---

[61] Yonan, "Toward a Fusion," 242.
[62] Yonan, "Toward a Fusion," 234.
[63] Yonan, "Toward a Fusion," 237-8.

privileging of "high art" paintings and sculpture over "decorative arts" (such as ceramics), as well as the post-*reconquista* privileging of Christian as the definitive marker of medieval Spain.

Islamic art history is perhaps inherently more aligned with a material culture approach due to many factors: by definition, it includes many cultures and many interpretations of Islam, and by practice, it encompasses a multiplicity of forms and objects infused with meaning. Yonan notes that scholars interested in non-Western societies "have for decades probed objects that fall well outside commonplace definitions of art."[64] An element that distinguishes the study of 'Islamic art' from other kinds of art historical disciplines, according to Islamic and Asian art historians Sheila S. Blair and Jonathan M. Bloom, is the variety of forms or artistic media used. This has led to some objects being determined to be of lesser value base on Western presumptions as evidenced in the hierarchy of value implicit in Western art historians valuation of 'fine art' over and above 'decorative art.' Thus, "much of what many historians of Islamic art normally study—inlaid metalwares, luster ceramics, enameled glass, brocaded textiles, and knotted carpets—is not the typical purview of the historian of Western art, who generally considers such handicrafts to be 'minor' or 'decorative' arts compared with the 'nobler' arts of architecture, painting, and sculpture."[65]

Addressing the difficulty of defining Islamic art, Grabar states: "'Islamic' does not refer to the art of a particular religion, for a vast proportion of the [objects] have little to do with the faith of Islam. Works of art demonstrably made by and for non-Muslims can be appropriately studied as works of Islamic art." Further, Grabar argues, the

---

[64] Yonan, "Toward a Fusion," 234.
[65] Sheila S. Blair and Jonathan M. Bloom, "The Mirage of Islamic Art: Reflections on the Study of an Unwieldy Field," *The Art Bulletin* 85, 1 (2003): 152.

"important point is that 'Islamic' in the expression of 'Islamic art' is not comparable to 'Christian' in 'Christian art.'"[66] Acknowledging the difficulty of an accurate definition, Grabar notes, "[i]f it exists at all, Islamic art would be one that overpowered and transformed ethnic or geographical traditions… As in the study of Gothic architecture or Baroque painting, one of the historian's problems becomes to distinguish what in a given moment is native and what belongs to the Islamic overlay, and to keep some sort of balance between the two components."[67]

Islamic art historian Mehmet Aga-Oglu clarifies that "Islamic art…is a composite art. It is a manifestation of a civilization and not of a culture. Although bound together by a single faith, the countries and the peoples of Islam do not constitute a single culture."[68] With this acknowledgment of diverse influences within specific regions it is therefore important to pay careful attention to the specific forms and imagery used in artworks within the particular mix of multiple cultural contexts.

The complexity of categorizing Islamic art is echoed by Blair and Bloom: "[T]he academic field of Islamic art has only a tenuous and problematic relationship with the religion of Islam. While some Islamic art may have been made by Muslims for purposes of the faith, much of it was not. A mosque or a copy of the Koran clearly fits everybody's definition of Islamic art, but what about a twelfth-century Syrian bronze canteen inlaid with Arabic inscriptions and Christian scenes?"[69] Specifying further, Blair and Bloom state that the term "Islamic" is inaccurate: "[M]ost scholars tacitly accept that the convenient if incorrect term 'Islamic' refers not just to the religion of Islam but to the

---

[66] Oleg Grabar, *The Formation of Islamic Art* (New Haven: Yale University Press, 1987): 1-2.
[67] Grabar, *Formation of Islamic Art*, 2.
[68] Mehmet Aga-Oglu, "Remarks on the Character of Islamic Art," *The Art Bulletin* 36, 3 (1954): 174.
[69] Blair and Bloom, "Mirage of Islamic Art," 152.

larger culture in which Islam was the dominant—but not sole—religion practiced ....[T]he term 'Islamic art' seems to be a convenient misnomer."[70]

Philosopher Ismail Al-Fārūqī lists seven names of Western scholars[71] who have made their reputation on "[d]ecades of fastidious scholarship and analysis of meticulous reconstruction, identification...that they were judging Islamic art by the norms and standards of Western art." Each scholar "held the erroneous assumption" that "Islam has impeded or restricted, and thereby impoverished" the artistic expression of Muslim people.[72] Given these misunderstandings, Al-Fārūqī asserts that "historians of Islamic art have unanimously judged that art by standards of Western aesthetics.[73]

Given the limitations and prejudices of art historical methodology on its own, material culture studies re-aligns analytical priorities to incorporate and acknowledge all objects within a culture as holders of cultural and artistic significance and value.

Methodological Application

This dissertation employs Prown's three-step methodological procedure for assessing and interpreting objects integrating methods of both material culture studies and art history. The three stages include:

1. *Descriptive analysis*— substantial analysis of physical dimensions, material, and articulation, analysis of content such as subject matter and a reading of overt representations, and formal analysis of object's configuration and visual character;
2. *Deductive analysis*—the relationship between the object and the perceiver, sensory engagement, intellectual engagement, and emotional response; followed by

---

[70] Blair and Bloom, "Mirage of Islamic Art," 153.
[71] Al-Faruqi lists Richard Ettinghausen, H. G. Farmer, M. S. Dimand, T. W. Arnold, E. Herzfeld, K. A. C. Creswell, and G. von Grunebaum.
[72] Ismail R. Al-Faruqi, "Islam and Art," *Studia Islamica*, 37 (1973): 82.
[73] Al-Faruqi, "Islam and Art," 83.

3. *Speculative analysis*—framing questions which lead out from the object to external evidence for testing and resolution.[74]

The fusion of material culture studies and art history into one methodology according to Prown allows for objects to be used "actively as evidence rather than passively as illustrations."[75] This combined methodology allows for study of cross cultural influences as evidenced in Late Medieval Iberian luster glazed ceramics objects decorated with a combination of religious motifs. Rather than approaching inter-religious interactions in Islamic ruled and Christian ruled Iberia through surviving texts and documents, material culture studies and art history create a way to evaluate and appreciate cultural cross-influences and combined imagery on decorative ceramic objects created for everyday use or courtly display.

Conclusions

By the middle of the eight century, Prince 'Ab al Rahman I of the Umayyad Dynasty of Syria, conquered and ruled most of Iberia which he called *Al-Andalus* in Arabic. The three names used to describe the Medieval Iberian Peninsula—*Al-Andalus, Hispania,* and *Sepharad*—reveal the complex mix of cultural and Muslim, Christian, and Jewish religious identities. In the thirteenth century, Muslim artisans fleeing political upheavals in Egypt and Persia brought significant contributions to the arts of *Al Andalus*. In particular, Muslim ceramicists brought traditional Islamic decorative motifs and specialized metallic glazing techniques enabling the creation of a new style of pottery in Iberia with dazzling reflective surfaces: luster glazed ceramics.

---

[74] Jules David Prown, "Mind in Matter: An Introduction to Material Culture Theory and Method," *Winterthur Portfolio* 17, 1 (1982): 7-10.
[75] Prown, "Mind in Matter," 1.

The most prolific production center of luster glazed ceramics emerged first in Islamic-ruled Málaga. However, due to ongoing religious wars between Muslims and Christians in Málaga, there was a dramatic decline in the number of Muslim artisans and thus a decline in the quantity of luster glazed ceramics produced there. In contrast, in Christian-ruled Valencia, religious wars between Christians and Muslims had subsided. Simultaneously, while conflict was increasing in Malaga it had decreased in Valencia. Therefore Valencia overtook and surpassed Málaga in production of luster glazed ceramics by both Muslim and Christian artisans.

The luster glazed ceramics reflect not only the brilliance and craftsmanship of the artisans who created them, but the decorative schemes also reflect the mix of their Muslim, Christian, and Jewish faiths. Previously overlooked by scholars as objects which have not been considered worthy of scholarly attention, studying luster glazed ceramics requires a methodology that combines both material culture studies and art history. This combined methodology allows for investigation of cross-cultural influences evidenced in Late Medieval Iberian luster glazed ceramics created for everyday use or courtly display which integrate Muslim, Christian, and Jewish decorative motifs.

Chapter Overview

Comprised of four parts, this dissertation addresses the historical evolution of how luster glazed ceramics began in Islamic cultures and how Muslim artisans brought this technique to Iberia. The second and third chapters examine the production of luster glazed ceramics and their changing religious motifs in fourteenth and fifteenth century Málaga and Valenica, respectively. The fourth and final chapter reflects upon the success of luster glazed ceramics with religious decorative schemes and the multiple factors that influenced its decline.

Chapter One covers development of the luster glazed ceramic art form. The development of luster glazed ceramics and their religious motifs addresses the origins and migration of Islamic and Christian artisans, the techniques and composition of forms, and the flourishing of luster glazed ceramics within Islamic Iberia.

Chapter Two examines Málaga, a key port city in Southern Iberia, in the Islamic ruled Kingdom of Granada. Málaga was the renowned production center of exquisitely crafted luster glazed ceramics such as the Alhambra Vases with their traditional Islamic imagery. Málaga was also a prolific distribution and export center of luster glazed ceramics where over time emerged lusterware with combined Islamic and Christian motifs. The decline of Málaga's luster glazed ceramics accompanied the fall of Islamic rulers in the Kingdom of Granada by 1492 along with the complete expulsion of Muslims from Iberia many years later by ascending Christian rulers.

Chapter Three investigates Valencia, a port city 300 miles northeast of Málaga, in the Christian reclaimed Kingdom of Aragon. Valencia became an even greater production and distribution center for luster glazed ceramics with religious motifs such as: (1) Traditional Islamic motifs; (2) Christian Family Coats of Arms; (3) Islamic and Christian motifs; and (4) Islamic and Jewish motifs. Due to multiple factors including political stability, Valencia eventually surpassed Málaga becoming the preeminent center of production and distribution of lusterware.

Chapter Four summarizes rise and fall of luster glazed ceramics and the multiple socio-political as well as religious factors which led to the decline of its production in Málaga and its success in Valencia.

Chapter One

The Development of Luster Glazed Ceramics

Origins and Migration

A few years prior to Prince 'Ab al Rahman I establishing himself to perpetuate the Umayyad Dynasty on the Iberian Peninsula, a captive Chinese artisan began teaching Abbasid craftsman in Bagdad a ceramic glazing technique that produced glittering metallic surfaces. Hirst explains that in 751 "several Tang Dynasty craftsmen including one named Tou Houang were kidnapped from their workshops" and then "brought to Baghdad where they were kept for eleven years, working closely with Abbasid craftsmen before they were released to return to China."[76] Though we can name one of the Chinese craftsmen who taught the skill of creating luster glazed ceramics to Muslim artisans in the Abassid Dynasty's new capital Bagdad, the names of subsequent creators of luster glazed ceramics by and large remain anonymous and unknown.

Extensive trade routes and ease of mobility within the Mediterranean region facilitated the migration of artisans and their wares. Muslim ceramicists brought luster glazing techniques to the northeast African region of Egypt's Fatimid Dynasty in power from 909-1171. By the tenth century, Abassid ceramic wares, including luster glazed works, were imported to Islamic Iberia. According to Mariam Rosser-Owen, Curator in the Victoria and Albert Museum's Middle Eastern Department, "[l]ocal production began at a later date, probably due to the transfer of the requisite technical knowledge from

---

[76] Hirst suggests that Muslim potters may also have moved to China (voluntarily or not) work and learn the craft there: "the only reason we know of Tou Houang at all is from his extant report to his government after he returned." Kris Hirst, "Islamic Lustreware: Origins and Techniques—Tang Dynasty Influences," *Archeology.about.com*, updated 1/18/16,
http://archaeology.about.com/od/islamicarchaeology/ig/Islamic-Lustreware-/Tang-Dynasty-Influences.htm#step-heading.

Timeline of Origins and Migration of Luster Glazed Ceramics			
Tang Dynasty Eighth Century China	Abassid Dynasty 751 Bagdad	Fatimid Dynasty 909-1171 Egypt	Nasrid Dynasty 1232-1487 Málaga
			Kingdom of Aragon 1238-1600s Valencia (includes Manises & Paterna)

Table 3. *Timeline of Origins and Migration of Luster Glazed Ceramics.*

Fatimid Egypt."[77] By the late thirteenth century, political upheavals in Egypt and Persia created vast diasporas of Muslim artisans and merchants who sought out the more politically stable climate of Islamic Iberia. Muslim ceramicists brought advanced glazing and firing techniques to the Iberian Peninsula enabling the creation of a new style of pottery in this region.[78]

Prior to Islamic conquest, indigenous Iberian artisans made pottery influenced by Roman, Visigoth and Byzantine styles considered "highly developed," as assessed by Guillermo Roselló Bordoy, historian and archeologist. Contending that the Muslim craftsmen mixed their skill with local artisans, Bordoy describes as a new Iberian "mixture of indigenous and Roman techniques with North African and oriental influences, a symbiosis, that lent new dimensions to art. Out of this amalgam would be born the ceramics of the Islamic epoch."[79] Throughout the centuries of Islamic rule and influence, Bordoy asserts there was an "enormous diversity" of Iberian ceramic centers

---

[77] Mariam Rosser-Owen, "Bowl: Historical Context," accessed December 28, 2015, http://collections.vam.ac.uk/item/O85365/bowl-unknown/.

[78] Political upheavals in Egypt and Persia in the early fourteenth century created a vast diaspora of Islamic artisans and merchants who sought out the more politically stable climate of Islamic Iberia.

[79] Roselló Bordoy, "The Ceramics of Al-Andalus," 97.

with multiple variations in decorative schemes and forms produced by skilled ceramicists throughout many locales.[80] By the thirteenth and fourteenth centuries, popular Iberian pottery styles included: (1) green and brown tin-glazed ceramics,[81] and (2) *cuerda seca* (which translates to 'dry rope') technique that evolved from the green and brown ware in which areas of different colors are separated by a painted outline of brown manganese; its effect is similar to that of cloisonné enameling.[82]

A third style emerged, that of the metallic luster glazed ceramics. By the thirteenth and fourteenth centuries in Islamic Iberia, patrons were no longer reliant on trade to obtain this style—artisans skilled in production of metallic luster glazed ceramics now lived in their midst. The quality of the craftsmanship flourished as described by a Anthony Ray, Curator at the Victoria and Albert Museum of London: "Lustreware of whatever quality required expert knowledge and special care was taken over anything made for a rich patron. Each piece bore witness to a very high level of technical skill, unrivalled anywhere in Europe at the time."[83] The Islamic ruled regions of the Iberian Peninsula became known as the site of expertly crafted luster glazed ceramics. According to Guillermo Rosselló Bordoy, the largest numbers of surviving luster glazed ceramics inscribed with religious motifs are directly linked to the cities of Málaga and Valencia.[84]

---

[80] Rosselló Bordoy, "The Ceramics of Al-Andalus," 98.
[81] Also referred to as 'green and manganese ceramics' as the element manganese when mixed in ceramic glaze and heated to high temperatures takes on a reflective brown hue. Rosselló Bordoy, "The Ceramics of Al-Andalus," 98.
[82] Rosselló Bordoy, "The Ceramics of Al-Andalus," 99.
[83] Anthony Ray, *Spanish Pottery 1248-1898* (London: Victoria & Albert Publications, 2000), 66.
[84] According to Rosselló Bordoy, other Iberian locales produced luster glazed ceramics: Calatayud, Saragossa, and Majorca in the Kingdom of Aragon, Toledo, Murcia, Alicante, and Badajoz in the Kingdom of Castile and Leon. Either these cities were more sporadic in their output of luster glazed ceramics than Málaga and Valencia, or their luster glazed ceramics did not survive in as great a quantity. Rosselló Bordoy, "Ceramics of Al-Andalus," 99.

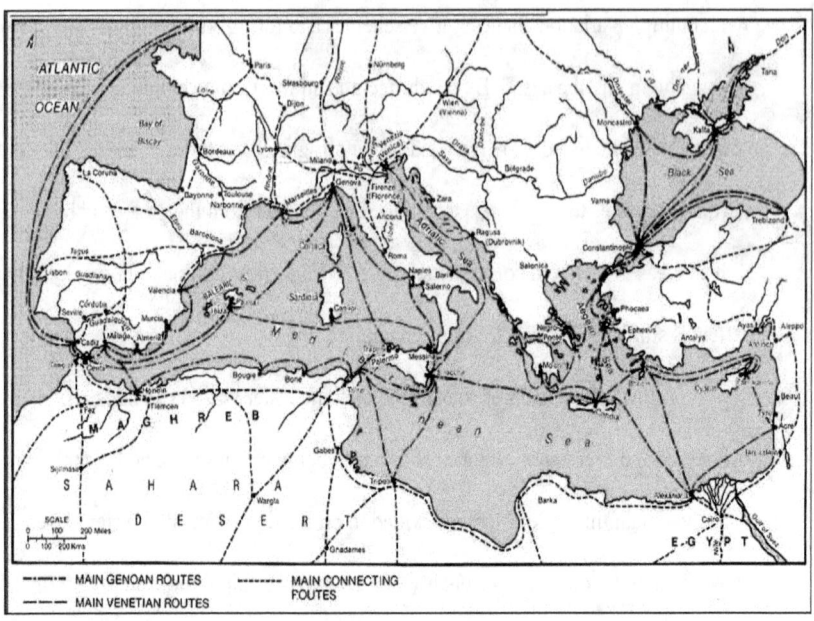

Map 5. *Main Mediterranean and Black Sea Routes in Medieval Times c. 1092.* [85]

Due to expert craftsmanship, lusterware from Al-Andalus became a highly sought after commodity by royals and the nobility within and beyond the Iberian Peninsula. Luster glazed ceramics from Iberia were exported from Islamic-ruled Málaga and from Christian-ruled Valencia to England, France, Italy, Egypt, Syria, Palestine, Asia Minor, and Turkey where they were much appreciated according to Architect and Archaeologist Leopoldo Torres Balbás.[86] Art historian Cristina Stancioui describes the fluid exchange of export and import: "[C]eramic wares utilized in domestic contexts were…commodities involved in long-distance exchange between Europe and the Middle East."[87]

---

[85] Tom Wukitsch, "Medieval Roman Economy," accessed December 18, 2016, http://www.mmdtkw.org/MedRomUnit0700-0PixList.html.

[86] Leopoldo Torres Balbás, "Bibliography of Spanish Muslim Art 1939-1946," *Ars Islamica* 15/16 (1951): 180.

[87] Cristina Stancioui, "Objects and Identity: An Analysis of Some Material Remains of the Latin and Orthodox Residents of Late Medieval Rhodes, Cyprus, and Crete" (PhD diss., University of California, Los Angeles, 2009), 26.

Numerous trade routes threaded throughout the Mediterranean basin made cross cultural exchanges possible (see map 5). According to Stancioui, "common decorative motifs" in ceramics including those "originating in Islamic repertoires" were prevalent throughout the Medieval Mediterranean.[88] Historian of art and archeology Anna McSweeney describes potters from the region of Valencia as being a "part of a western Mediterranean movement in tin-glazed ceramics, which exploited new connections in international trade in the thirteenth and fourteenth centuries."[89] Among this vast system of trade and exchange, the luster glazed ceramics reflecting the mix of Muslim, Christian, and Jewish traditions within late medieval Iberia became some of the most highly sought after commodities.

Many import records list specific names of royal and noble patrons of luster glazed ceramics. For example, historian Summer S. Kenesson cites an example of an inventory of imports "from Portsmouth, England, dating from 1289, [which] mention the arrival of some lusterware from Málaga en route to Eleanor of Castile, wife of Edward I of England. Two others refer to Málagan ceramics, one from Kent in the early fourteenth century and another from Collioure, in the Narbonne region [of France], from 1297. Furthermore, the famous traveler Ibn Battuta wrote in 1350 that 'at Malaqa there is manufactured excellent gilded pottery, which is exported thence to the most distant lands.'[90] The records for Eleanor of Castile are quite detailed: "the clerk of the port of

---

[88] Stancioui, "Objects and Identity," 27.
[89] Anna McSweeney, "The Green and the Brown: A Study of Paterna Ceramics Oriental and African in *Mudéjar* Spain" (PhD diss., University of London, 2012), 19.
[90] Summer S. Kenesson, "Nasrid Luster Pottery: The Alhambra Vases," *Muqarnas* 9 (1992): 93-94.

Sandwich reported the arrival of "42 bowls, 10 dishes and 4 earthenware jars of foreign colour (*extranei coloris*)."[91]

Many names of patrons are not recorded though the existence of this ceramic ware in so many parts of the contemporary world attests to their widespread popularity. According to Christina M. Nielsen, Curatorial Fellow at the Art Institute of Chicago, it may be that a scarcity of gold in the fifteenth century throughout Europe and the Mediterranean Basin led to the greater popularity and therefore production of lusterware ceramics: "Their glittering appearance appealed to aristocratic users during the fifteenth century, when gold was in short supply."[92] Lisa Golombek, Curator Emeritus of Islamic Art at the Royal Ontario Museum, pinpoints a key question: "the determination of an object's 'social index.' For whom was it made? Sometimes this information is conveniently written somewhere—in inscriptions or texts—but more often we have to make intelligent guesses."[93]

Techniques, Materials, and Designs

Creating luster glazed ceramic ware required not only the expertise of skilled Muslim artisans but also upon a complex infrastructure and an extensive support network. Golombek describes how potters with technical skills and materials also needed support industries for their enterprise as well as the right social and economic environment: " Ceramics require an enormous pyramid of trades and skills to allow a fine luxury object worthy of the name of 'art' to be produced: sourcing and preparation of

---

[91] Rosser-Owen, "Bowl: Historical Context."
[92] Christina M. Nielsen, *Devotion and Splendor Devotion and Splendor: Medieval Art at the Art Institute of Chicago* (Chicago: Art Institute of Chicago, 2004), 25.
[93] Lisa Golombek, "The Language of Objects in the Islamic World: How we Translate and Interpret it: Commentary on the Symposium Roundtable "Objects of and in Islamic History" and Culture."*Ars Orientalis* 42 (2012): 16.

body, glaze, and pigment materials, the making of tools, the provisions and skills related to the construction and operation of kilns, and the means of transport to market." Thus, Golombek asserts, the production of a "luxury pottery type" such as luster glazed ceramics "required time and money."[94]

The process of transforming raw clay into hardened lustrous ceramic ware involves multiple steps. Unglazed raw clay ranges in hue from gray to brown to reddish brown depending upon the soil composition. Local variations of soil composition can actually help scholars pinpoint the production locale of certain ceramic wares. In one case, one of the bowls studied in this dissertation ("fig. 7") soil analysis was used to pinpoint the bowl's site of production as Málaga. Rosser-Owen notes that the discovery of a mineral called schist[95] definitively determined that curators had incorrectly classified the bowl as "Valencian ware" until 1983 when "analyses conducted on it in that year identified the provenance of schist inclusions in the clay body as the Málaga region."[96]

Mastering the skills to create ceramic ware involves understanding of techniques, tools, materials, and a lot of time. Techniques include learning how to shape and form the clay either in flat slab form for tiles or wheel thrown pottery for round or cylindrical forms followed by multiple finishing steps. Records show that wheel thrown pottery, which allows for consistent replicable forms, was revived in Córdoba under Islamic rule. Anthropologists James L. Boone and Nancy L. Benco explain the factors that by the end of the Late Roman Iberian period (circa 450 to 711) "wheel-made pottery production had nearly ceased and was only revived again in the late ninth and tenth centuries, during the

---

[94] Golombek, "Language of Objects in the Islamic World," 16-17.
[95] Schist is a "metamorphic crystalline rock that has a closely foliated structure and can be split along approximately parallel planes." *Merriam-Webster.com*, s.v. "schist," accessed August 21, 2016, http://www.merriam-webster.com/dictionary/schist.
[96] Rosser-Owen, "Bowl: Historical Context."

consolidation of the Umayyad Caliphate centered in Córdoba, perhaps as a response to the conditions under which population densities had again increased and trade networks reformed to the point that such industries could be supported."[97]

The hand-made ceramic ware industry of this era required an intense investment of time and energy. In order to complete any ceramic object such as a luster glazed plate necessitated multiple stages. First, the plate needed to dry and harden. If the plate needed any manipulation, such as puncturing holes in the rim (to make it suitable for displaying it on a wall), an artisan needed to partially dry the plate to the leather hard phase. Once completely dry, the plate was placed into a kiln—a special furnace that reaches high temperatures to harden clay products—a process called firing. The normal process for producing a ceramic plate involves a two step firing process: the first, called a 'bisque firing,' hardens and seals the porous clay surface.[98] Then artisans painted liquid glazes—comprised of the elements of glass (sand, soda, and lime)[99] and other minerals for coloration—on the 'bisque' plate. Then a second firing would fuse the elements and minerals into a vitreous coating which makes the object not only water proof but also, according to Rosselló Bordoy, "kept the clay from absorbing the odors of food and giving off an unpleasant taste."[100]

In order to get a metallic luster surface on ceramic ware, artisans in Iberia developed a different process—with two layers of glazing which each required their own separate firing. A catalogue from the Metropolitan Museum in New York explains the

---

[97] James L. Boone and Nancy L. Benco, "Islamic Settlement in North Africa and the Iberian Peninsula," *Annual Review of Anthropology* 28 (1999): 66.
[98] See **Appendix 2** for complete definitions of ceramics production.
[99] *OxfordDictionaries.com*, "glass," accessed August 09, 2016, http://www.oxforddictionaries.com/us/definition/american_english/glass.
[100] Rosselló Bordoy, "The Ceramics of Al-Andalus," 99.

evolution of a multi-step process: "The first step in the technique of Spanish lusterware was to glaze a fired piece of clay with an undercoat of white and then paint the design in deep blue. Details could be obtained by *sgraffito*—a method of scratching the surface to reveal the white undercoat. Luster, a mixture of silver and copper oxides to which red ocher, silt, and vinegar were added, was applied only after a second firing." Depending upon "the proportions of the mixture of oxides" luster glazes resulted in tones "ranging from pale gold to deep reddish copper." It was this second coat of a luster glaze applied to an already glazed and fired ceramic object "that distinguishes Hispano-Moresque wares from other contemporary ceramic production."[101] Rosselló Bordoy notes that the recipes for mixtures of oxides were carefully guarded by "a complex secret process employed by specialized artisans" giving the process of producing a "metallic luster or golden sheen" to ceramic ware an aura of mystery.[102]

In the Nasrid era in the Kingdom of Granada, luster glaze on ceramic ware blossomed with what Rosselló Bordoy describes as a "splendid resurgence of the use of gold. The introduction of cobalt oxide added blue to the spectrum of glazes; indeed, blue and gold would be the characteristic of Nasrid ceramics" in Málaga. This luster glazed ceramic ware "was not only widely distributed but quickly imitated by Valencian potters."[103]

Islamic culture in this epoch influenced the forms created in Málaga pottery workshops. Large ceramic ware was needed for the Islamic 'family style' custom of preparing, serving, and consuming food on communally shared bowls and plates, as

---

[101] Timothy Husband, "Valencian Lusterware of the Fifteenth Century: Notes and Documents." *The Metropolitan Museum of Art Bulletin* 29, 1 (1970): 20.
[102] Rosselló Bordoy, "The Ceramics of Al-Andalus," 99.
[103] Rosselló Bordoy, "The Ceramics of Al-Andalus," 101.

opposed to smaller individual plates or bowls. The forms of luster glazed ceramics vary from complete dinner sets to individual bowls, deep dishes, jugs, platters, and serving plates. Boone and Benco explain the pervasive impact of Islamic culture upon multiple cultures in the region: "[t]he adoption of Islamic social practices in both urban and rural contexts may be signaled by the appearance of distinctive glazed, polychrome food vessel serving forms-conical bowls, platters, pitchers, tureens-in the late ninth and tenth centuries…These forms are indicative of the adoption of communal forms of food service and hospitality. Although they may not constitute proof of Islamization in all cases, they are clearly associated with medieval Muslim food preparation and serving practices."[104]

The Islamic Context

A first rationale explaining why luster glazed ceramics took hold and flourished in Medieval Islamic cultures—especially in Islamic Iberia—stems from Islamic law called *hadith* which according to Cragg, translates from Arabic meaning 'news' or 'story.'[105] *Hadith* are records of sayings and daily practices of the Prophet Muhammad.[106] In conjunction with the Qur'an, the word of God, the *hadith* have been codified and appended with commentaries that serve as a foundation of Islamic law and moral guidance.[107] As such, *hadith* are the major source of guidance for Muslims.[108]

---

[104] Boone and Benco, "Islamic Settlement," 66.

[105] "The term *Hadith* derives from the Arabic root *ḥ-d-th* meaning "to happen" and so "to tell a happening," "to report," "to have, or give, as news," or "to speak of."…From *Hadith* comes the Sunnah (literally, a "well-trodden path"—i.e., taken as precedent and authority or directive), to which the faithful conform in submission to the sanction that *Hadith* possesses and that legalists, on that ground, can enjoin. Tradition in Islam is thus both content and constraint, *Hadith* as the biographical ground of law and Sunnah as the system of obligation derived from it." *Encyclopædia Britannica Online*, s. v. "Hadith," accessed March 18, 2016, https://www.britannica.com/topic/Hadith.

[106] These sayings were not transcribed by the Prophet Muhammad but rather are "collections of reports claiming to quote what he said verbatim on any matter." Gordon D. Newby, "Hadith," *A Concise Encyclopedia of Islam* (Oxford: One World, 2002), 95.

[107] Juan Eduardo Campo, "Hadith," *Encyclopedia of Islam* (New York: Facts on File Publishing, 2009), 50.

Interpretation of *hadith* is a dynamic and ongoing process among Muslim scholars. According to Aga-Oglu, the particular *hadith* passage many scholars cite is a warning that states: "He who drinks from gold and silver vessels drinks the fire of hell."[109] This passage has often been cited as the proscription which required artisans to create dinner ware from materials other than metal. Boone and Benco ascribe causality to this *hadith* passage as the proscription that in essence created the proliferation of luster glazed ceramic ware in Islamic cultures stating "human ingenuity produced the famous Hispano-Muslim luster pottery as a substitute for…gold and silver vessels."[110] Luster glazed ceramic ware thus conveys the image of opulence with its glittering reflective glaze while adhering to Islamic law.

Secondly, a pragmatic rationale posits that financial considerations influenced the popularity of luster glazed ceramics. As archeologist Kevin Greene explains, cost may have been a factor for the proliferation and popularity of ceramic ware "[b]ecause fewer people between the Roman period and early modern Europe could afford comprehensive metal table services, decorated glazed earthenware (whether Byzantine white ware, Islamic luster ware, Italian maiolica, Delft, or Staffordshire slipware) did find a place on 'respectable' tables."[111]

Alternatively, a third rationale for the proliferation of luster glazed ceramics posited by Aga-Oglu argues that the development of metallic luster glaze for ceramic ware was not necessarily aligned with devout observation of Islamic law; rather, the

---

[108] *OxfordDictionaries.com*, s.v. "Hadith," accessed February 23, 2016, https://en.oxforddictionaries.com/definition/hadith

[109] Aga-Oglu, "Character of Islamic Art," 185.

[110] Boone and Benco, "Islamic Settlement," 66. Author's note: they mistakenly ascribe the proscription to the Qu'ran instead of *hadith*.

[111] Kevin Greene, "Late Hellenistic and Early Roman Invention and Innovation: The Case of Lead-glazed Pottery," *American Journal of Archaeology* 111, 4 (2007): 657.

technical achievement of luster glazed ceramics emerged more out of Islamic artisans' pursuit of creating and reflecting beauty in all things. Aga-Oglu explains: "It is a fallacy, in my opinion, to theorize that luster was invented for imitative purposes to safeguard the religious virtues of luxury-loving [Muslims].... The invention of luster was a technical achievement of high merit in the history of ceramic art, and was an original contribution devoid of pretentious meaning."[112] Ziauddin Sardar, Chair of the Muslim Institute in London, notes that even among Islamic clerics and jurists there is not universal agreement on the veracity of all *hadith*; while there may be different categories of *hadith* ranging from 'authentic' to 'good' to 'weak,' "there is no overall agreement: different groups and different individual scholars may classify *hadith* differently."[113] As evidence of this diversity of interpretation, Aga-Olu cites examples of Muslim rulers renowned for their vast collections of gold and silver food vessels; these rulers were clearly not concerned with detailed interpretation of *hadith* applying to their daily habits of food consumption.[114] Instead, many luster glazed ceramic objects seem to have been prized by collectors solely based upon their beauty. Muslim artisans devoted considerable effort to produce these objects of beauty—and Muslim, Christian and Jewish patrons seem to have commissioned these ceramics in large quantities and in many regions.

    These luster glazed ceramic objects inscribed with religious images serve a dual purpose of utility on which to serve food and ornament to inspire contemplation and reflect beauty in all things. Artisans devised this complex series of processes to create

---

[112] Greene, "Late Hellenistic and Early Roman Invention and Innovation," 190.
[113] Ziauddin Sardar, *The Future of Muslim Civilisation* (London: Croon Helm, 1979), 26.
[114] Sardar, *Future*, 26.

objects that were both functional and elegant. Nielsen describes this "golden pottery" as "striking in appearance and prized" both for its practical utility and opulent elegance.[115]

Many of the large dishes were clearly intended for display, and perhaps to inspire devotion, as evidenced by their piercing with often two small holes in the rim (done during the leather hard phase of production before the initial firing). Alice Wilson Frothingham, historian and curator at the Hispanic Society of America, confirms both the preciousness of these objects and the desire to display them on the wall as a work of art when noting that these luxury items were so prized they were often listed in an owner's will: "Large dishes like this can have holes in their rim, so they can be hung on a wall."[116] When placed on display, their reflective surfaces were a reminder of the infinite beauty of the divine. As Frothingham summarized, "The notion of earthenware as a luxury item for display was one that had originated in the Islamic world."[117]

Aesthetic beauty was not mere superficial decoration in Islamic cultures as Tazim R. Kazzam, historian of religions, explains: "In Islam, there is an intimate relationship between the search for beauty and the refinement of one's nature. The aesthetic pursuit of beauty has an ethical impulse since the artist cultivates a way of being in the world that intuits and senses minutely the inherent complexity and intricacy of the universe."[118] Dodds and Walker explain the meaning and content implicit in religious decorative schemes: "visual sources contributed to the development of ingenious and complex aniconic ornament that engaged the viewer in a contemplative rather than an empathetic

---

[115] Nielsen, *Devotion and Splendor,* 26.
[116] Alice Wilson Frothingham, *Catalogue of Hispano-Moresque Pottery in the Collection of the Hispanic Society of America* (New York: Hispanic Society of America, 1936), xxx.
[117] Frothingham, *Catalogue,* 28.
[118] Tazim R. Kazzam, "Ethics and Aesthetics in Islamic Arts." *Islamic Arts and Architecture* (2011), accessed December 28, 2015, http://islamic-arts.org/2011/ethics-and-aesthetics-in-islamic-arts/

relationship, which distinguishes Islamic religious arts from those of Christians."[119] Thus, rather than using figurative imagery to convey meaning as much of Western Christian arts do, Islamic art objects with intricately decorated surfaces inspire meaning achieved through internal insight and reflection.

Thus, what might appear as 'merely decorative' to a non-Muslim viewer could be infused with religious significance to a Muslim viewer. Golombek posits the question as "whether the arts of the Islamic object behave any differently than those of other cultures."[120] Yet her follow-up question assumes "detachment" between these objects and those who view or use them; she asks, "does the detachment of most Islamic objects from religious involvement make them very different in their reception by Islamic society than, say, Christian objects within medieval Europe?"[121] This question implies that only objects used in communal worship are intrinsically "religious" whereas these objects seek to integrate spiritual reflection into daily life much as prayer in Islam is integrated into daily rhythm five times a day.

As Kazzam explains: "[i]t is often said that art in Islamic cultures exists not just for the sake of art itself, but to act as a constant reminder of the beauty of God's presence. Both nature (God's creation) and the arts (human creations) are understood as intimations of Divine mercy." And further that there is a direct link between and the divine: "In Islamic arts, there is a connection between beauty and the sacred. The Qur'an is filled with verses exhorting human beings to witness the endless marvels of God's

---

[119] Dodds and Walker, "Introduction," xx.
[120] Golombek, "Language of Objects in the Islamic World," 16.
[121] Golombek, "Language of Objects in the Islamic World," 16.

creativity…Islamic arts thus involve the thoughtful contemplation and remembrance…of Creator, creation, and creativity."[122]

Using gold to inscribe Arabic verses—understood to be "the language of God"—was an ultimate means of celebrating and elevating sacred words in Islamic cultures. Menocal cites the tradition of using gold to emblazon religiously inspired poetry at an annual poetry competition in Mecca: "winning poems would be embroidered in gold on banners and then hung on display at the ancient shrine."[123] Thus, the golden hued calligraphic inscriptions on ceramic objects could be seen as a more permanent way of 'embroidering' and conveying meaning.

Dodds and Walker describe insights gained from study of these ceramic works: "these objects can provide passage not only to visual and tactile experiences of beauty and power but also to an understanding of how the Muslims of *al-Andalus* saw themselves; they allow us to understand the meaning of courtly patronage and display for the Islamic princes of the Iberian Peninsula and to see the search for identity hidden within…each work of art. For these were more than opulent adornments intended to impress—though on one level they were certainly that; they were also the means by which the Muslim rulers of *al-Andalus* created a visual setting for themselves on the western frontier of Islam."[124] Thus the objects combined with their settings created a larger message anchored not only in a political display of power but even more fundamentally anchored in proclaiming their Muslim faith.

To summarize, a distinctive quality of Islamic art is the use of patterns of decoration on all surfaces—whether on small objects or large architectural spaces: every

---

[122] Kazzam, "Ethics and Aesthetics."
[123] Menocal, *Ornament of the World*, 62.
[124] Dodds and Walker, "Introduction," xix.

surface provides the opportunity for ornamentation. The decorative patterns employed are not arbitrary but rather are often intricate and interlocking systems of vegetative or geometric symbols employed to inspire devotion and reflection upon the vastness of the divine. Order in this world reflects infinite divine order. The highly decorated surfaces of luster glazed ceramic wares paralleled the patterns of highly decorated surfaces of their surroundings: rugs, floor tiles, mosaics on the walls, and carved *muqarnas* on the ceilings found in the homes of the wealthy and the common gathering places from the mosques to the bath houses. [125] These intricate designs reflected a geometric order and an order of shapes from the natural world which formed a coherent message, a reflection of *Allah* in all things.

Underscoring this message was calligraphy, often in highly stylized formats, to literally spell out the words of the teachings and principles of Islam. Kazzam explains the spiritual aspirations of calligraphers: "The artist seeks to become like the pen in the Hand of God along with those who pledge allegiance to the prophet and are thus guided by God: "The Hand of God is upon their hands"…The calligrapher's prayer is to become an instrument in the Hand of God through perfect surrender, concentration, and devotion." Further, notes Hazzam, the stylized calligraphy utilized often on the luster glazed ceramic objects was meant to be seen as a part of a larger decorative ornamentation: "Calligraphy, the most distinctive and cultivated of Islamic arts, has aptly been described as the geometry of the spirit."[126]

---

[125] *Muqarnas* are "a form of architectural ornamented vaulting in Islamic architecture, the geometric subdivision of a squinch, or cupola, or corbel, into a large number of miniature squinches, producing a sort of cellular structure, sometimes also called "honeycomb" vaults from their resemblance to these." James Stevens Curl, *A Dictionary of Architecture and Landscape Architecture* (Oxford: Oxford University Press, 2006), 31.

[126] Kazzam, "Ethics and Aesthetics."

In addition to geometric and natural patterns of ornamentation, there are multiple examples within different Islamic cultures of the artistic representation of animals and human figures. While the key text of Islam, the Qur'an, does not prohibit visual depictions of figures, many supplemental Muslim texts such as *hadith* do forbid such representations especially of the prophet Muhammad.[127] What the Qur'an does prohibit is idolatry as Nielson summarizes: "Although the Qur'an contains no direct prohibition against the use of images, various parties within Islam held strong iconoclastic views and eschewed the representation of figures within holy sites; for this reason, calligraphic script and other decorative motifs dominated Islamic art."[128] While figurative or representational art was forbidden within a religious or worship setting, in most Islamic cultures there are plentiful examples of representational art on objects of daily living including some of the metallic luster glazed ceramics. Umayyad patrons did not demur from the representation of the figure, although its use was restricted. The figure is often integrated into an overall surface decoration of interlace and foliage to that is poised ambiguously between formal device and bearer of meaning."[129]

These distinctions are not widely understood in the West by those who are not conversant with Islamic scholarship.[130] Western scholars' assumptions regarding a unilateral ban on figurative representation in all of Islam also affect the ability to see work such as the ceramic ware with images of the human world on their own terms.

---

[127] There are several examples of Persian manuscripts from the tenth through sixteenth centuries which contain actual images of the Prophet Muhammad. Nada Velimirović, "Contested Bodies: The Emergence and Destruction of Figurative Imagery Counter to Traditional Understandings of Faith,"(unpublished manuscript, April 16, 2011), Microsoft Word file.

[128] Nielsen, *Devotion and Splendor,* 19.

[129] Dodds and Walker, "Introduction," xx.

[130] The issue permissible portraits of Muhammad has appeared in recent years in an episode of the cartoon *South Park* and the political drawings of Danish and French cartoonists; these episodes seem to have fueled more misinformation, fear, and censorship than to have improved a more nuanced and complex public understanding of Islam.

When scholars do pay attention to figurative representations in 'Islamic art' they are susceptible to making sweeping generalizations across cultures based upon their own preconceptions. With this cautionary statement in mind, the ceramic works with figurative images will be examined in their particularities without making overarching statements about Islamic figurative art in general.

While luster glazed ceramics originated in countries which were primarily under Islamic rule, by the late medieval period of Islamic Iberia there was a combination of cultures including Muslims, Christians and Jews. This particular mix influenced the work of the artisans and patrons who were not only from this region but, as it has been shown, ranged throughout Europe and the Mediterranean basin.

Conclusions

In 751, a few years prior to the establishment of an Islamic Emirate in Iberia, a captive Chinese artisan taught Muslim craftsman in Bagdad a technique fo galzing ceramics that produced glittering metallic surfaces. Due to the existence of extensive trade routes and ease of mobility within the Mediterranean region, Muslim artisans and their newly produced luster glazed ceramic wares migrated with relative ease. Muslim ceramicists from Bagdad brought luster glazing techniques to Egypt and then later to Islamic Iberia. Among a vast system of trade and exchange, the luster glazed ceramics reflecting the mix of Muslim, Christian, and Jewish traditions in late medieval Iberia became some of the most highly sought after commodities.

Creating luster glazed ceramic ware in Iberia required not only the expertise of skilled Muslim artisans but also upon a complex infrastructure and an extensive support network. In order to get metallic luster surfaces on ceramic ware, artisans in Iberia developed time intensive process requiring multiple layers of glazing each of which required their own separate firing. Luster glazes from pale gold to deep reddish copper were combined with cobalt blue on a white background to create the characteristic color scheme for traditional Islamic luster ware in Málaga; glaze recipes and motifs were soon imitated and produced by Muslim artisans in Valencia.

Among the rationales which explain why luster glazed ceramics took hold and flourished in Medieval Islamic Iberia, many credit an Islamic law, called *hadith*, which was understood as a proscription against eating or drinking from gold or silver vessels. A second rationale states that luster ware ceramics was simply less expensive than costly metal dinnerware. An alternate rationale cites the aesthetic value in Islamic culture to reflect beauty in all things as the driving force for Muslim artisans' technical achievement of luster glaze for ceramics. A distinctive quality of Islamic art is the use of patterns of ornamentation on all surfaces—whether on small objects or large structures. Intricate and interlocking decorative patterns including flowers and vegetative motifs, geometric shapes, and calligraphy combine to inspire devotion and reflection upon the vastness of the divine.

Chapter Two

Málaga's Emergence as an Economic, Artistic, and Cultural Center

This chapter examines the emergence of the most prolific production center in Iberia of luster glazed ceramics in Málaga, a port city on the southern coast which was a vital economic, artistic, and cultural hub in the Islamic ruled Kingdom of Granada. Unified and established first by Prince Ibn Ahmar, the Nasrid Dynasty ruled of this region from 1232 until 1487. Kenesson describes the importance of Málaga during Nasrid rule: "Ibn Ahmar was well able to exploit the natural benefits of the region's geography and made the most of the trading opportunities he had with the Christians of Castile and the Almohads of North Africa,[131]even using one as an ally against the other as it suited his diplomacy. Although Granada was [the] capital, Málaga as a major port, became the artistic and cultural center of the province."[132] Due to the continuing onslaught and warfare of Christian rulers trying to "re-conquer" this last stronghold of Islamic Iberia, Málaga was "one of the best fortified coastal cities in the western Mediterranean."[133] In this highly embattled environment, traditional Islamic arts flourished.

Málaga is located 100 kilometers east of Gibraltar on the southern coast of Iberia facing the Mediterranean Sea. As a key commercial port, a lucrative trade of multiple local goods such as wines, textiles, ironwork, figs and other produce thrived.[134] Málaga's location afforded easy transit of multiple wares and access to multiple trade routes. Extensive documentary evidence, such as inventories of goods at ports throughout

---

[131] Buresi and El Aallaoui, *Governing the Empire*, 3.
[132] Kenesson, "Nasrid Luster Pottery," 93-94.
[133] Rosser-Owen, "Bowl: Historical Context."
[134] Husband, "Valencian Lusterware,"12.

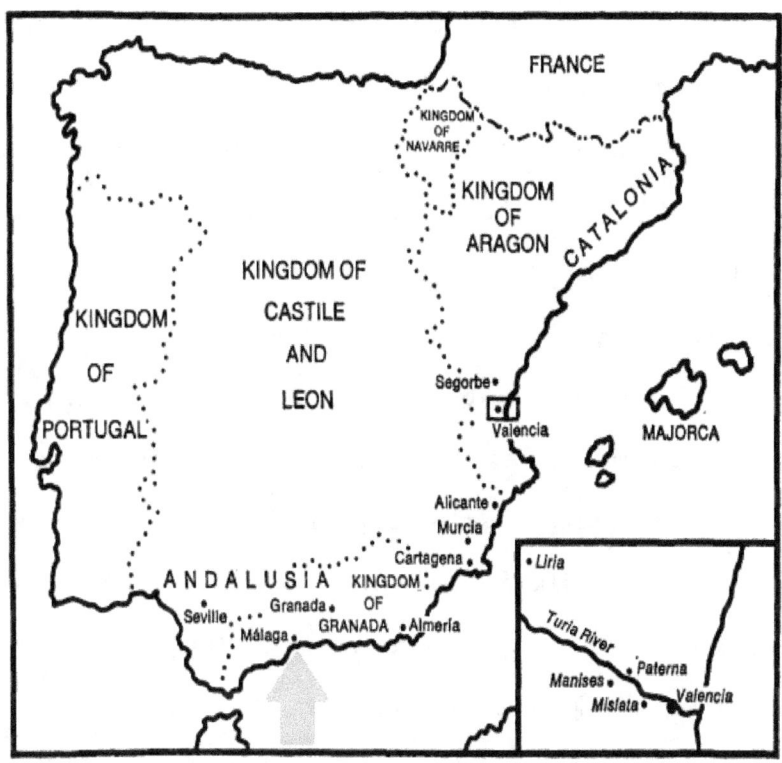

Map 6. *Kingdoms of the Iberian Peninsula during the fourteenth and fifteenth centuries highlighting Málaga.*

Europe and the Mediterranean, substantiates that Málaga was the hub of trade and commerce for the region of Granada.[135] Rosser-Owen corroborates this citing: "ample literary, documentary and archaeological evidence that Málaga's products were exported throughout Europe and the Middle East." She adds that a "good deal of Málaga ware has been found at the medieval site of Fustat in Cairo, Egypt. A cobalt-blue and lustre dish found there has the word *Malaqah* inscribed within its footring… The fact that the place of manufacture was recorded on goods made for export attests to Málaga's international renown at the time."[136]

---

[135] Kenesson, "Nasrid Luster Pottery," 93.
[136] Rosser-Owen, "Bowl: Historical Context."

Torres Balbás refers to archeological excavations finding numerous fragments of luster glazed "Hispano-Moresque" ceramics found during archeological excavations: "they are almost always of the luster type of the fourteenth and fifteenth centuries… exported from Málaga to Egypt, where they were much appreciated, as well as to Syria, Palestine, Asia Minor, and Turkey."[137]

Muslim Artisans

As Málaga was connected to shipping routes throughout the Mediterranean basin, it was easy for Muslim artisans to immigrate here and for the import of required materials for their craft. Kenesson describes this region as a "constant traffic" in both goods and people."[138] Several factors explain why Málaga was so well suited to become a major production and export center of luster glazed ceramics: (1) As a port city, its geographic proximity linked it directly to the Mediterranean; (2) Infrastructure for large scale production of ceramic ware was already in place as Rosser-Owen notes that Málaga was well-known as a center of ceramic production since the tenth century;[139] (3) Skilled artisans with the "requisite technical knowledge" of how to combine oxides to make luster glazes arrived from Egypt when the Fatimid Empire fell in 1171; and (4) Additional political upheavals in Egypt and Persia in the early fourteenth century created a vast influx of more Muslim artisans and merchants who sought out the more politically stable climate of Islamic Iberia.[140] The renown of the artisans was not only within the region but spread to other regions quickly as Nielson explains: "The Islamic craftsmen of Andalucia, in southern Spain, excelled in the production of luxury ceramics… The

---

[137] Balbás, "Bibliography of Spanish Muslim Art," 180.
[138] Kenesson, "Nasrid Luster Pottery," 93-94.
[139] Rosser-Owen, "Bowl: Historical Context."
[140] Rosser-Owen, "Bowl: Historical Context."

famous lusterware from the coastal town of Málaga was originally made for the Nasrid nobility [the rulers of the Kingdom of Granada] but soon became especially appreciated abroad."[141]

Multiple sources attest to the quality of craftsmanship of the luster glazed ceramics which emerged from Málaga. The earliest reference dates to the late thirteenth century as explained by Timothy Husband, Curator at the Metropolitan Museum: "Around 1274...the writer Ibn Said from Granada made special mention of Málagan lusterware."[142] Rosser-Owen quotes a 'geographical treatise' from 1337 which said of Málaga: "It is famous for its luster pottery, the like of which is not known elsewhere."[143] Husband notes the most often cited reference: "In 1350 Ibn Battuta from Tangiers said that a beautiful lustered pottery was made in Málaga and exported to the most remote countries."[144] Kenesson also attests that "the famous traveler Ibn Battuta wrote in 1350 that 'at Malaqa[145] there is manufactured excellent gilded pottery, which is exported thence to the most distant lands.'"[146]

Alhambra Vases: Traditional Islamic Motifs

Representing a monumental achievement in technical skill and aesthetic beauty, the luster glazed Alhambra Vases created in Málaga replicate traditional Islamic decorative schemes from the past.[147] The examination of luster glazed ceramic objects begins with three vases known as Alhambra Vases which Rosselló Bordoy claims

---

[141] Nielsen, *Devotion and Splendor*, 26.
[142] Husband, "Valencian Lusterware," 12.
[143] Rosser-Owen, "Bowl: Historical Context."
[144] Husband, "Valencian Lusterware," 12.
[145] 'Malaqa' is the Arabic spelling of what we now refer to as Málaga.
[146] Kenesson, "Nasrid Luster Pottery," 93-94.
[147] The luster glazed ceramic ware with combinations of imagery from different faith traditions emerged later in Málaga and are more evident in Valencia.

epitomize "the highest manifestations of the art of Nasrid ceramics."[148] Their name stems from the Alhambra Palace; these vases are believed to have been created to display in palace niches.[149]

As stated earlier, the Nasrid Dynasty coalesced in the context of Islamic rulers' diminished hold on the Iberian Peninsula which Menocal described as "the wolves howling mightily at the door."[150] Dodds and Walker infer that "the creation of arts for the Nasrids became part of the fashioning of a public image: defiant statements of artisitic grandeur in a land nearly lost to Islam. It is as if the Nasrids felt they could defy a rapidly encroaching Christian rule through the power of an old an potent visual culture."[151] Menocal contends that the Alhambra Palace, built by Nasrid rulers in their capital Granada, serves to "monumentalize the inevitability of loss."[152] All of the ten known Alhambra Vases are a monumental size and according to Rosser-Owen, they are "the largest Islamic ceramics in existence"[153] varying between 1.2 and 1.7 meters in height.[154]

According to Rosser-Owen, Málaga, which was the major Nasrid Dynasty's center for production of luster glazed ceramics, "was where the magnificent 'Alhambra Vases' were manufactured."[155] Kennesson explains the historical process of deduction: "luster ceramics were as important as exports as they were in decorating the Alhambra palace of the Nasrid kings in Granada, so both functions for the industry are possible and

---

[148] Rosselló Bordoy, "The Ceramics of Al-Andalus," 354.
[149] A total of ten Alhambra Vases exist today in differing conditions; an eleventh vase was destroyed in 1936. See **Appendix 3. Alhambra Vases**.
[150] Menocal, "Visions," 5.
[151] Dodds and Walker, "Introduction," xxi.
[152] Menocal, "Visions," 7.
[153] Rosser-Owen, "Bowl: Historical Context."
[154] Or, varying from 3 feet 11 inches to 5 feet almost 7 inches in height.
[155] Rosser-Owen, "Bowl: Historical Context."

must be taken into consideration when determining the location of the industry's center. For the sake of reducing costs, the production site could also have been used for shipping the products overseas, and a seaside factory would therefore make the most sense. Only the occasional piece destined for Granada would then have to undergo the risk and expense of being sent by mulecart over the mountains."[156] She adds that "[w]hile it is certain that there were potters working in Granada, it is improbable that they produced anything other than household goods and tiles." [157]

Kenesson addresses the implications of the complex creation process: "[l]ittle is known about how these vases were made…a few points can be concluded on the basis of how ceramics are produced today. The vases were certainly molded in parts, and then probably fired as a single piece. …due to the complicated process of making such vases, the number of vases produced in a given period of time would be limited, especially if the workshops were making other objects as well and so sharing the use of the kilns between these vases and other more marketable items." [158] Kenesson notes that the monumental vases may have originated "from a single workshop…The lack of demand would certainly contribute to a limited production, possibly on a commission basis."

However, Kenesson cautions: "[i]t is also possible that many more were made than are extant today, and indeed, fragments of similarly shaped and decorated objects exist. Even so, the immense cost of creating objects like the vases would suggest that some care was taken in their preservation."[159] Triki corroborates these findings stating that "[m]ost scholars attribute their provenance to the city of Málaga" adding that "shards

---

[156] Kenesson, "Nasrid Luster Pottery," 95.
[157] Kenesson, "Nasrid Luster Pottery," 95.
[158] Kenesson, "Nasrid Luster Pottery," 95.
[159] Kenesson, "Nasrid Luster Pottery," 95.

found in the Alhambra suggest that many more existed" and that "[l]usterware production is supported by archeological finds."[160]

The surviving Alhambra vases share the same large distinctive shape, derived from ancient amphora and described by Rosselló Bordoy as "the shape traditional for storage jars." He adds, "because of their size and unwieldy contours we must assume that these vessels were more decorative than practical. The ovoid body, with its narrow base and tall neck, is provided with flat, triangular handles that could only be ornamental, since they offer no handhold."[161] Triki specifies the shape copying that of wine jugs— they are "like traditional *tinajas*[162] (large wine jars made in the tenth and eleventh centuries in Andalusia and North Africa). The grooved cylindrical base swells into a broad pear shape and a long ribbed neck opens into a protruding lip; two wing shaped handles, some decorated, join the body to the neck."[163] Studio potter and historian of pottery Alan Caiger-Smith notes that the shape and monumental scale of these vases is an anomaly in the production style of late fourteenth to early fifteenth century Málagan luster glazed ceramics.[164]

Assessment of the following three Alhambra Vases will follow Prown's methodology using descriptive, deductive, and speculative analysis. The following monumental Alhambra Vases combine the following imagery: (1) Floral and vegetative motifs; (2) Geometric symbols; (3) Calligraphic inscriptions in Arabic. The intricately intertwined decorative patterns combine forms from both the natural world as well as

---

[160] Hamid Triki, "The So-Called Alhambra Vases," *Qantara Mediterranean Heritage*, http://www.qantara-med.org/qantara4/public/show_document.php?do_id=398
[161] Rosselló Bordoy, "The Ceramics of Al-Andalus," 354.
[162] Translates from Spanish to 'jug.'
[163] Triki, "Alhambra Vases."
[164] Alan Caiger-Smith, *Lustre Pottery: Technique, Tradition and Innovation in Islam and the Western World* (London: Faber and Faber, 1985), 89.

geometric shapes in order to form a coherent message: a reflection of the divine in all things.

Figure 1, *Alhambra Vase (1)*

The first object, figure 1, *Alhambra Vase (1)* is also referred to as the "Palermo Vase" due to its being discovered, notes Rosselló Bordoy, in excavations in Sicily,[165] and its current location in Palermo, Sicily.

Descriptive Analysis

Alhambra Vase (1), on display at the *Galleria Regionale della Sicilia*, Palermo, was created in the late thirteenth century and stands at a height of 128 centimeters.[166] The color scheme contains two tones: an intense bronze-tinged gold and a creamy white. Decorative elements include multiple combinations of floral and vegetative motifs intertwined with geometric symbols. The boldest decoration is the Arabic calligraphic inscription on the central band.

Handles

The flat curved handles arch up from the upper body of the jug shape with a pattern of a white octagonal lattice on a dark bronze background with both seven- and eight-petal white flowers at the center. Interlinking the octagonal shapes are equidistant bronze pointed cross shapes. Two small cylinders of clay topped with ball span the gap between the top of the handle and the neck of the vase.

---

[165] Rosselló Bordoy, "The Ceramics of Al-Andalus," 354.
[166] Or, four feet and just over two inches.

Figure 1. *Alhambra Vase (1)*, Probably Málaga, late thirteenth century, height: 128 cm. Galleria Regionale della Sicilia, Palermo

Neck

The neck of the vase is described by Rosselló Bordoy as having "vertical bands separated by ribs."[167] The vertical strips alternate between wider strips and thinner 'ribs.' The wide strips (twice the width of the ribs) contain varied lace-like filigree articulated in bronze on a white background with suggestions of flower and vine forms. The thin strips contain an interlocking knot shape; these rise to the lip of the vase to raised curling shapes reminiscent of the tops of Doric columns. Under the rim are more scalloped shapes.

Juncture of neck and body:

There are four horizontal bands described by Rosselló Bordoy as "graduated rings at the juncture of the neck and the body."[168] These alternate between chevron patterns and interlocking knots echoing the thinner vertical strips on the neck.

Body:

There are five horizontal bands of decoration on the body—the top two and bottom two bands frame the widest band filled with Arabic calligraphy. Undulating leaf and vine patterns separated by thick bronze-toned lines comprise the top two bands. The first band below the calligraphy repeats a similar undulating leaf and vine design with curling patterns comparable to *fleur de lys*. The bottom band is twice the width of the leaf band above it and contains a repetitive arched shape rendered in bronze on white which is reminiscent of fish scales; at the center of the arch the interior space is filled with a lighter gold color fan shape.

---

[167] Rosselló Bordoy, "Ceramics of Al-Andalus," 354.
[168] Rosselló Bordoy, "Ceramics of Al-Andalus," 354.

Figure 2. *Alhambra Vase (1)*: **Detail**

The boldest decoration is the widest horizontal central band with what Rosselló Bordoy states is "a large inscription in the graceful characters of the Granadine *Kufic*,[169] repeating endlessly the watchword *al-mulk*, kingship or dominion."[170] The repeated phrase *al-mulk* is a contraction of a longer phrase "*al-mulk l'illah* ('Power is with God')" as Triki explains.[171] The white background is filled completely with a repeated geometric swirl shape adding a dynamic contrast to the right angles in the calligraphic script.

Deductive Analysis

According to Victor Borges, Senior Sculpture Conservator at the Victoria and Albert Museum, this *Kufic* script corresponds with other calligraphic inscriptions used in

---

[169] Kufic is "an early angular form of the Arabic alphabet found chiefly in decorative inscriptions." *OxfordDictionaries.com*, s.v. "Kufic," accessed August 18, 2016, http://www.oxforddictionaries.com/us/definition/american_english/kufic
[170] Rosselló Bordoy, "The Ceramics of Al-Andalus," 354.
[171] Triki, "Alhambra Vases."

the Alhambra Palace. Borges asserts that *Kufic* calligraphy "usually refers to quotations from the Holy Qur'an [and] consists of a combination of square and angular lines with bold circular forms."[172]

Speculative Analysis

Most scholars agree that the function of a vase such as this was primarily decorative not utilitarian. As Triki summarizes, "The function of these vases is another riddle—their size, weight, and fragility would exclude any functional use. They seem to have been originally placed in large alcoves, as found in the Nasrid royal residences."[173] While specific intent cannot be ascribed, it seems their purpose was to make a strong and lasting visual impact. As Caiger-Smith notes, "few other pots in the world make such a strong physical impression."[174]

The calligraphic inscription on this *Alhambra Vase (1)*—produced in the last outpost of late Medieval Islamic Iberia, in the Kingdom of Granada—may infer a hearkening back to not only the origins of Islamic rule in Iberia but the origins of Islam. Rosselló Bordoy suggests type of calligraphy links it to historical antecedents: "[t]his vase may belong to moment marked by a return to an archaic *Kufic*."[175] Further study is needed, states Rosselló Bordoy, because these "austere characters" have "not been thoroughly studied."[176] According to Rosselló Bordoy, "the presence of *al-mulk* recalls the caliphal ceramics…in its moment of greatest splendor, when the simple articulation

---

[172] Victor Borges, "Nasrid Plasterwork: Symbolism, Materials & Techniques," *Victoria and Albert Museum Conservation Journal*, 48 (2004), accessed March 25, 2016, http://www.vam.ac.uk/content/journals/conservation-journal/issue-48/nasrid-plasterwork-symbolism,-materials-and-techniques/.
[173] Triki, "Alhambra Vases."
[174] Caiger-Smith, *Lustre Pottery*, 101.
[175] Rosselló Bordoy, "Ceramics of Al-Andalus," 355.
[176] Rosselló Bordoy, "Ceramics of Al-Andalus," 355.

of this word was enough to define a political reality."[177]   Thus, the calligraphic message asserts and echoes the dominion claimed in the early days of the Umayyad Caliphate in Iberia—which itself was a claiming of direct lineage to the foundations of Islam and the Prophet Muhammad.

Figure 3, *Alhambra Vase (2)*

The second object, figure 3, *Alhambra Vase (2)* is also referred by two other names: as the "Fortuny Vase" due to its discovery and purchase in the nineteenth century by Spanish painter Mariano Fortuny[178] and the "Hermitage Vase" due to its current location at the Hermitage Museum in St. Petersburg, Russia.[179]   Its bronze stand, evident in two other of the Alhambra Vases, is a nineteenth century addition designed by Fortuny himself and was inspired by the Fountain of the Lions at the Alhambra Palace.[180] No records have been found to confirm how the original vases were displayed.

Descriptive Analysis

Alhambra Vase (2), on display at the State Hermitage Museum, St. Petersburg Russia, was created in the early fourteenth century and stands at a height of 117 centimeters.[181] The color scheme contains two tones: an olive-tinged gold and a creamy

---

[177] Rosselló Bordoy, "Ceramics of Al-Andalus," 355.

[178] Also known as Mariano José María Bernardo Fortuny y Marsal. *Encyclopædia Britannica Online*, s.v. "Mariano Fortuny," accessed August 18, 2016, https://www.britannica.com/biography/Mariano-Fortuny-Spanish-painter-1838-1874.

[179] Rosselló Bordoy states Fortuny bought it in 1871, "when it was serving as the base for the holy water font in the del Salar church in the province of Granada. It was purchased from the sale of Fortuny's collection in Paris in 1875 by the Russian A. P. Basilevsky. In 1885 the vase entered the collection of the Hermitage as part of Basilevsky's collection, which was bought by the Russian government." Rosselló Bordoy, "Ceramics of Al-Andalus," 357.

[180] "Vase: Label," Smithsonian Insitution: Freer Gallery, accessed December 5, 2015, http://www.asia.si.edu/collections/edan/object.php?q=fsg_F1903.206a-b&bcrumb=true. The other two vases with stands by Fortuny are known as the Freer and Simonetti Vases (see Appendix 3, Alhambra Vases).

[181] Or, three feet ten inches.

Figure 3. *Alhambra Vase (2).* Probably Málaga, early fourteenth century, height: 117 cm. State Hermitage Museum, St. Petersburg

white. Decorative elements include combinations of floral and vegetative motifs intertwined with geometric symbols. Arabic calligraphy is inscribed on a central band, in medallions above that band, and on the vase handles. Figurative imagery is intimated in what appear to be two hands—one on each of the handles.

Handles

The two flat curved handles arch up from the upper body of the jug shape with an upraised hand on each. These stylized hands are a motif which appear often in Islamic art and are understood to be a sacred reference; the 'sacred hand' symbol is known by many names: (1) The hand of God; (2) *Khamsa* or *Hamsa*; (3) The hand of Fatima. Each of these names refers to the same symbol; for purposes of clarity, in this dissertation they shall be referred to as the sacred hand. See the following *Deductive Analysis* for discussion of etymologies of the names referring to this symbol.

The hands appear as almost duplicates. Though each hand is painted in gold on a white background with four fingers raised up and a smaller 'thumb' curling to the right, slight variations differentiate each hand. For example, the hand on the left has two white circles with a gold dot in the center inscribed on the palm while the hand on the right has an inverted white drop shape on its palm.[182] Further, each hand is supported by a leaf shape which with differing calligraphic inscriptions which Rosselló Bordoy suggests can be "interpreted as cuff from which the hand is emerging." The left handle "is embellished with arabesque decoration" and the right handle "bears an epigraphic motif that could be read as 'benediction.'"[183]

---

[182] See figure 4, *Alhambra Vase (2): Detail*.
[183] Rosselló Bordoy, "Ceramics of Al-Andalus," 356.

The background consists of a white glaze dappled with small gold dots with small undulating gold wave shapes framing the indented wrists of the hands. At the top of the handles appear broken embellishments—perhaps remnants of the same kind of two small cylinders of clay topped with ball which span the gap between the top of the handle and the neck of on *Alhambra Vase (1)*.

Neck

The neck of the vase contains wide vertical strips alternating with thin plain gold strips which rise to the lip of the vase (as with the previous vase) to form curling shapes like the tops of Doric columns. The wide strips contain varied lace-like filigree articulated in gold on a white background with suggestions of flower, leaf, and vine forms.

Juncture of the neck and body

There are four horizontal bands ringing the juncture of the neck and the body. These alternate between two thin bands of chevron patterns and two wider bands of an endless interlocking knot pattern. Of note, this juncture is almost identical to the previous Alhambra Vase.

Body

The decorations on the body of this vase are unique among Alhambra Vase. As Rosselló Bordoy explains, its decorative scheme "presents a double central band with inscriptions, bordered above and below by areas ornamented with arabesques. The double band does not appear in any other vases of this type."[184]

---

[184] Rosselló Bordoy, "Ceramics of Al-Andalus," 356.

With a total of four bands, the double band of calligraphy is framed by a top row of arabesques[185] an ornamentation suggestive of calligraphy, and a bottom row of intertwining leaf and vine patterns. Executed in white glaze on a gold background, the upper band of calligraphy is described by Rosselló Bordoy as presenting "a composition of concentric circles, each bearing the word 'pleasure.'"[186] The spandrels between the circles contain graceful white shapes that appear as dashes and interlaced curves. On the lower band of calligraphy the color scheme "offers a chromatic contrast to the band above" using gold glaze for calligraphy on a white background. As opposed to the "austere" calligraphy on the previous vase, the *Kufic* script here is more ornate. Rosselló Bordoy explains the content: "the word 'health' appears repeatedly in Granadine Kufic, without the usual article." In between the fluid script, leaves and vines twine on a background inscribed with light gold swirls.

Deductive Analysis

One of the most striking elements of *Alhambra Vase (2)* are the upraised hands embellishing the handles as it is the only one of the ten extant Alhambra Vases with this complete decoration. The Alhambra Vase known as the 'Jerez Vase' with only one handle intact is the only other Alhambra Vase with a 'sacred hand' decoration. (See "Jerez Vase" in Appendix 3.)[187] As mentioned earlier, these stylized 'sacred hands' are a motif which appear often in Islamic art and this motif is known by multiple names: (1) *The Hand of God*; (2) *Khamsa* or *Hamsa*; (3) *The Hand of Fatima*. The following is an

---

[185] "Arabesques are an ornamental design consisting of intertwined flowing lines, originally found in Arabic decoration." *Oxford Dictionaries.com*, s.v. "arabesque," accessed August 19, 2016, http://www.oxforddictionaries.com/us/definition/american_english/arabesque.
[186] Rosselló Bordoy, "Ceramics of Al-Andalus," 356.
[187] Three of the surviving Alhambra Vases have no handles: the Freer Vase, the Osma Vase and the Simonetti Vase (see Appendix 3, Alhambra Vases). There is no way to know what decorative schemes their handles contained.

Figure 4. *Alhambra Vase (2):* **Detail**

etymology of each phrase showing that each name refers to the same kind of sacred hand and connection to the divine. The 'sacred hand' can be called:

(1)

The Hand of God: The 'sacred hand' is also known as 'the hand of God,' according to Kenesson, and this term "has a long and complicated history." She adds that it could symbolize "royal authority or the divine power of God." Further, a passage in the Qur'an that refers to the hand of God reads "'that His Grace is entirely in His hand, to bestow it on Whomsoever He wills.' This implies that Allah's hand is the instrument by which

Faith, Grace, and Fortune are meted out to believers, a particularly attractive interpretation considering the princely function of the vases. This is doubly convincing if it can be agreed that the five straight fingers of the hand are meant to represent the word 'Allah' in Arabic."[188] A contemporary calligraphic example shows this form: اللّٰه.[189]

(2) *Hamsa*: Islamic historian Amira El Azhary Sonbol explains the etymology of called *hamsa*, another name for 'sacred hand,' as meaning 'five' in Arabic. The symbol of a raised hand with closed fingers has multiple associations with many Mediterranean cultures.[190]

(3) *The Hand of Fatima*: Sonbol explains another name for the 'sacred hand' is 'the Hand of Fatima' within Muslim cultures—so named for the daughter of the Prophet Muhammad.[191] In addition, historian Joseph Shadur and artist and art historian Jehudit Shabur note that this "favorite Muslim talisman" became a part of practical Jewish lore in North African and Middle Eastern Jewish cultures due to the correlation between the five fingers and the number five "which stands for the Ineffable Name" of God.[192]

Speculative Analysis

This combination of 'sacred hands' within the context of the natural and calligraphic forms suggests an interrelationship of God as shaper of the natural and human worlds. Having such an image in the royal setting of the Alhambra Palace could serve to reinforce the link between a ruler's power and divine power.

---

[188] Kenesson, "Nasrid Luster Pottery," 96.

[189] "Arabic form of the word 'Allah,'" accessed August 17, 2016, http://sufi-mystic.net/Allah99.htm

[190] Some spell *hamsa* in "the Romanized *khamsa*" format. Amira El Azhary Sonbol, *Beyond the Exotic: Women's Histories in Islamic Societies* (Syracuse: Syracuse University Press, 2005), 357.

[191] Also referred to "within Levantine Christian cultures as 'the Hand of Mary.'" Sonbol, *Beyond the Exotic*, 358.

[192] Joseph and Jehudit Shadur, *Traditional Jewish Papercuts: An Inner World of Art and Symbol* (Lebanon, New Hampshire: University Press of New England, 2002), 92.

The calligraphic message which twines 'pleasure' with 'health' on *Alhambra Vase (2)* may be a blessing or wish. The message seems intended to reflect upon either the present Nasrid rulers or of being goals attained in a future paradise. This differs from the historically rooted message of inferring a legacy of dominion in the prior vase. Perhaps the message of this vase is seen as a fulfillment of *Alhambra Vase (1)*.

Figure 5, *Alhambra Vase (3)*

The third object, figure 5, *Alhambra Vase (3)* is also referred to as the "Freer Vase" as it is part of the collection of the Smithsonian Institution's Freer Gallery in Washington, D.C. Of the surviving Alhambra Vases, it has sustained the most damage with only the body remaining: breakage includes missing handles and neck, large gouges in the surface area as well as diminishment of the luster glaze. As with the previous vase in figure 3, the *Alhambra Vase (3)* in figure 5 has a nineteenth century addition in its bronze stand intended to reference the lion fountain in the Alhambra Palace designed by Mariano Fortuny.[193]

Descriptive Analysis

Alhambra Vase (3), on display at the Smithsonian Institution's Freer Gallery in Washington, D.C., was created in the late fourteenth to early fifteenth century and stands at a height of 77.2 centimeters.[194] Visible surface damage consists of large gashes of missing glaze, worn off luster glaze, and truncated handles and neck. The color scheme contains two hues: opaque white and deep cobalt blue. To contemporary viewers, another hue now incorporated in the vase is the reddish brown tone of underlying

---

[193] Fortuny is reported to have found and purchased this vase from a tavern in Granada. "Vase: Label," Smithsonian Insitution: Freer Gallery, accessed December 5, 2015, http://www.asia.si.edu/collections/edan/object.php?q=fsg_F1903.206a-b&bcrumb=true.

[194] Or, two feet and just over six inches.

Figure 5. *Alhambra Vase (3)*. Probably Málaga, late fourteenth-early fifteenth century, height: 77.2 cm. Smithsonian Institution: Freer Gallery, Washington, D.C.

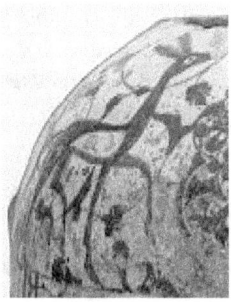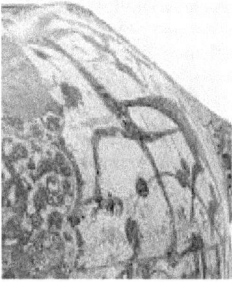

Figure 6. *Alhambra Vase (3):* **Detail**

earthenware where glaze has chipped off. Decorative elements include a combination of floral and vegetative motifs, geometric symbols, cursive Arabic calligraphy, and figurative representation of deer.

Body

Despite the damage, three bands of decoration are clearly distinguishable delineated by a delicate cobalt blue line (as opposed to the broad gold bands used to separate decorative schemes in prior vases). In the top band a white background contains images rendered in cobalt blue. Two deer face each other with a large oval mass of intertwining leaves, flowers, and vines in between them. Both deer have delicate tendrils of vines and leaves inscribed around them as well. Each deer body appears almost as a line drawing with it blending blend into the background with a large white leaf shape on its midsection. The deer on the right may actually have antlers as it seems to have more than just leaves and vines protruding from its head.

The central band of calligraphy inscribe in cobalt blue against the white background encircles the vase without interruption and is the smallest band on the surface of the vase—roughly a third the height of the top band. The poetic inscription is clearly identifiable, and as translated by Curator in Islamic Art, Massumeh Farhad, it reads:

> *O thou onlooker who art adorned with the splendor of the dwelling*
> *Look at my shape today and contemplate: thou wilt see my excellence*
> *For I appear to be made of silver and my clothing from blossoms*
> *My happiness lies in the hands of he who is my owner, underneath the canopy.*[195]

Its flowing cursive style, as Borges explains, is named *Nashkid-Thuluth* calligraphy.[196] The fluid lines of Arabic script echo the graceful lines used to delineate the floral and vegetative decorations as well as the lithe deer forms (see "fig. 6").

The bottom largest band of decoration comprised of a cobalt blue eight-pointed star offset by a white background centered under an arch of stylized curling tendrils and leaves. The star contains what appears to be a flower at its center with a geometric pattern of lines, partial stars, and dots radiating to its outer edges.

Deductive Analysis

The prominence of the eight pointed star on *Alhambra Vase (3)* reinforces the reminder that these vases were meant to be seen in the wider context of the Alhambra Palace. According to Borges, the eight pointed star was a motif often used in Nasrid art and at the Alhambra it was used as a part of decorative schemes on plaster walls and wooden ceilings.[197] Borges describes the vastness of the Alhambra as "a world of luxury and comfort, obtained through a combination of splendid architecture and formally designed gardens with numerous fountains and pools. The main architectural features within the buildings are ceramic mosaics, plasterwork and carved wooden ceilings all profusely decorated, reflecting the Islamic tendency to cover all surfaces with complex

---

[195] Massumeh Farhad, "Vase," Freer Gallery of Art, Smithsonian Institution, http://www.asia.si.edu/collections/edan/object.php?q=fsg_F1903.206a-b
[196] Borges, "Nasrid plasterwork."
[197] Borges, "Nasrid plasterwork."

ornaments,…blended together with subtle light effects, carpets, curtains and hanging textiles."[198]

Similarly, the style of the calligraphic inscription on *Alhambra Vase (3)* corresponds with one of the styles of calligraphy used to decorate other surfaces of the Alhambra Palace. Borges explains: "*Nashkid-Thuluth* calligraphy [cursive style] is a more elegant style used…as a reference to poetic quotations."[199] Farhad notes that the calligraphic inscription is unique among the existing Alhambra vases because it "makes the vase speak in the first person. Like…other inscriptions that survive in stucco at the Alhambra palace, this one asks the viewer to contemplate the beauty of the object and its setting."[200]

Speculative Analysis

As noted, Farhad assumes the luster glaze of this vase has been rubbed off by the wear of time. The original luster glaze on the vase may be referred to by the poem inscribed on the central band of decoration as it states, "*I appear to be made of silver.*" Based on numerous existing pottery fragments at the Alhambra Museum, the color scheme of white, cobalt blue, and luster would have been, according to Rosselló Bordoy, "the usual color scheme of the Alhambra vases."[201]

The poetic inscription incites the "onlooker" to reflect upon how they are situated "in the splendor of the dwelling" while being cognizant of mortality: "*Look at my shape today and contemplate.*" The poem encourages remembering "he who is my owner" with whom "my happiness lies." As such, this poem could address subjects of the King

---

[198] Borges, "Nasrid plasterwork."
[199] Borges, "Nasrid plasterwork."
[200] Farhad, "Vase."
[201] Rosselló Bordoy, "Ceramics of Al-Andalus," 356. Another vase with this intact color scheme, referred to as the "Antelope Vase," resides in the Museum of the Alhambra (see **Appendix 3**).

as well as the King equally reminding them that they all reside "in the hands of he who is my owner, underneath the canopy" of Allah.

More than the prior examples, *Alhambra Vase (3)* requires an imaginative leap to try to imagine its original appearance. As Farhad summarizes, "[i]ts present state only hints at its former appearance, as it must have been among the most magnificent of all of the late Alhambra vases."[202]

Dishes: Combining Islamic and Christian Motifs?

The following two luster glazed bowls show combinations of both Islamic and Christian motifs. Notably, the bowls include figurative representation—in the first of humans and animals, and animals in the second. As mentioned earlier, while many Westerners assume that all Islamic arts must be aniconic, or lacking in figurative imagery, there is a rich history throughout many Islamic ruled cultures and regions of Muslim artisans depicting animal and human forms. There following are two examples.

Figure 8. *Bowl with a Horseman Spearing a Serpent.*

The first object for examination is in figure 8, a *Bowl with a Horseman Spearing a Serpent.* Málaga is the assumed site of production—though this has not been definitively proven.

Descriptive Analysis

Bowl with a Horseman Spearing a Serpent, created in the late fourteenth or early fifteenth century, measures a width of 44 centimeters and a depth of 7.6 centimeters[203] and resides on display in Gallery 307 of the Metropolitan Museum in New York City. Damage to its surface includes chipped glaze revealing reddish earthenware underneath

---

[202] Farhad, "Vase."
[203] Or, a width of just over 17 inches a depth of 3 inches.

Figure 7. *Bowl with a Horseman Spearing a Serpent.* Probably Málaga, late fourteenth or early fifteenth century, width: 44 cm, depth 7.6 cm. Metropolitan Museum, New York City

Figure 8. *Bowl with a Horseman Spearing a Serpent*: Detail

in two areas: (1) just below the center to the left a series of chips near the horseman's stirrup; and (2) along the rim several chips—the largest on the lower left. Otherwise, the imagery is well preserved. The color scheme contains four hues: a creamy white, reddish brown, cobalt blue, and gold luster. Decorative elements include: (1) Vegetative motifs; (2) Geometric symbols; and (3) Figurative imagery of both humans and animals. The vegetative motifs provide a dynamic backdrop for this active scene. A series of limbs rise from one slender trunk in the center of the bottom rim; these limbs and tendrils connect behind the figures twining around the serpent, horse, and rider providing a lively backdrop. Each branch culminates in broad leaves creating a stylized canopy.

Three concentric circles of gold and blue glaze from the outer to inner rims provide the most evident geometric motif. In each consecutive pairing, the blue circles appear wider. On a part of the outer rim, four small coats of arms appear in oval disks. The *sgraffito* technique —when an artisan scratches through a darker glaze to reveal the white underglaze— renders other geometric shapes such as circles on the rider's armor, squares for the horse's blanket, and repeated half circles to define the serpent's scales and the texture of the leaves. Additionally, the stippled reddish brown dots on the white background provide another geometric element and hearken to a similar technique used on *Alhambra Vase (2)* on the handles as a backdrop for the sacred hands.

Figurative motifs include the horseman, his horse, the serpent, and another figure standing behind the rider. The rider and horse fill the center of the bowl in a dynamic composition where the coiled serpent frames the left and lower curve. A spear appears raised in the rider's left hand at the moment before it is plunged into the mouth of the giant serpent whose length is greater than that of the rearing horse. A smaller human figure stands behind the horse and rider with his feet perched near the serpent's tail while he raises a large shield and spear; while we can only see his left eye it appears to either be closed on looking down. All of the other figures' eyes are visible and most notably, both of the horse's eyes, circled in white, appear wide open as the horse comes face to face with the serpent.

Deductive Analysis

The composition of this scene includes several details that ground it historically. A *Metropolitan Museum of Art Bulletin* from an exhibition at The Cloisters describes the rider as wearing "a late fourteenth-century costume called a *gipon*"[204] and the smaller figure is described as a page wearing "a turban, short trousers, and leggings of the same period."[205] Ironically entitled "Valencian Lusterware of the Fifteenth Century," this 1970 publication attributes production of this bowl to Valencia. Attribution for *Bowl with a Horseman Spearing a Serpent* now reads "probably Malaga."

According to the aforementioned *Metropolitan Museum of Art Bulletin*, the image inscribed on this bowl in luster glaze may be inspired by the legend of St. George and the dragon.[206] Many consider the third century story of the martyrdom of St. George to be an exclusively Christian story, however, as historians of Islamic cultures Hovannisian and Sabagh explain that "Saint George is something of an exception among saints and legends, in that he is known and revered by Muslims, while being venerated by Christians throughout the Middle East, from Egypt to Asia Minor." Further, they explain, "His stature in these regions derives from the fact that his figure has become somewhat of a

---

[204] *Gipon* is a variant spelling of *jupon* "a close-fitting tunic, usually padded and bearing heraldic arms, worn over armor." *Dictionary.com*, s.v. "jupon," accessed: August 21, 2016, http://www.dictionary.com/browse/jupon

[205] Husband, "Valencian Lusterware," 20.

[206] Husband, "Valencian Lusterware," 20.

composite character mixing elements from Biblical, Quranic, and folkloric sources…He is said to have killed a dragon near the sea in Beirut, for which a Saint George Bay was built under his name."[207] Thus, both Muslim and Christians could venerate this object if as a possible image of St. George.

Speculative Analysis

There are elements, however, which remain as yet unidentified with this bowl. For example, there is uncertainty as to whether this is St. George or perhaps a representation of local dragon folklore.[208] Historian Oya Pancaraglu's work on "Dragon Slayer" images in Anatolia (modern day Turkey) may yield additional connections of analogous use of imagery between Muslim and Christian artisans.[209] In addition, on the outer rim, there are four small coats of arms which have yet to be identified.[210] Perhaps most significantly, further study including new scientific methods for sampling the composition of the clay could definitively determine the production site of *Bowl with a Horseman Spearing a Serpent*—methods which have been used on the following object.

---

[207] Richard G. Hovannisian and Georges Sabagh, *Religion and Culture in Medieval Islam* (Cambridge: Cambridge University Press, 2000), 109-110.

[208] Iberian folklorist Rick Chaffee chronicles stories of dragons from northern Spain including a *culebre* described as a "dragon-like creature, or a snake with two bat-like wings, that exhales fire and sulfur." Rick Chaffee, "Spanish Mythology," *Cultural Folklore, Mythology & Creationism in the Americas* (2012), accessed August 19, 2016, https://rickunioninstitute.wordpress.com/2012/11/16/spanish-spain-mythology/

[209] "The image of a figure on horseback impaling a large serpent or "dragon" was reincarnated over many centuries in medieval Anatolia, each reincarnation affirming the iconographic stability and contextual adaptability of the image. …Appearing on amulets, coins, icons, secular courtly decoration, and in funerary settings, the equestrian dragon-slayer assumed multiple and parallel identities in Christian and Muslim contexts. These identities intersect, in turn, with analogous narratives of sainthood and heroism in which the dragon slayer plays a distinct role in forging associations between traditions." Oya Pancaroğlu, "The Itinerant Dragon-Slayer: Forging Paths of Image and Identity in Medieval Anatolia," *Gesta* 43:2 (2004): 15.

[210] Husband, "Valencian Lusterware," 20.

Figure 9. *Bowl*

The next *Bowl* in figure 9 is a more conical shape and is the only luster glazed ceramic piece in this chapter proven to have been created in Málaga.

Descriptive Analysis

This capacious *Bowl* created between 1425 to1450 measures a width of 51.2 centimeters and a depth of 20.1 centimeters [211] and resides on display in the Victoria and Albert Museum in London. The bowl is in excellent condition with only a couple of small chips of glaze missing from its center (on the ships' main mast). The color scheme almost replicates the prior bowl with four glaze tones: a creamy white, reddish brown, cobalt blue, and gold luster. Decorative elements include: (1) Geometric motifs; and (2) Figurative imagery.

Simple geometric motifs in three concentric bands delineate the top rim of the bowl. The first reddish brown band contains a chevron pattern delineated in white followed by bands of gold and cobalt blue glaze. The *sgraffito* technique renders other geometric shapes such as the rigging on the masts, texture on the sails, the beams of wood on the ships' hull, as well as the scales on the large fish underneath the ship. Additionally, the small reddish brown swirls which fill the white background provide another geometric element and hearken to a similar technique used as a backdrop for the large calligraphic inscription on *Alhambra Vase (1)*. On this *Bowl*, the repeated geometric swirl shapes create a dynamic setting its floating ship. Finally, five crescents comprised of interlocking white arabesques on a reddish brown background appear to press inward toward the ship.

---

[211] Or, a width of or just over 20 inches and a depth of just over 7 inches.

Figure 9. *Bowl.* Málaga, 1425-1450, width: 51.2 cm., height: 20.1 cm. Victoria and Albert Museum, London

Figure 10. *Bowl*: Detail

The explicit figurative motif appears underneath the ship where four "large-bodied fishes" appear to be swimming. Each fish is depicted with precision—each with one large eye visible and their mouths slightly open. One fish faces left while the other three face right. As the furthest fish on the left swims to the left, its tail crosses with the fish to its right making a kind of cross shape. The implicit figurative scheme is the ship itself—though no humans are visible on board. Though the fore sail remains furled, the ship's main and aft sails swell and the five small pennants ripple as if billowing in a strong breeze. The family crest emblazoned upon the main sail appears to bear the form of an equidistant cross in the center.

Deductive Analysis

As described by Rosser-Owen, this bowl, while shaped by Muslim artisans, makes explicit reference to Christian symbolism. The ship depicted is "a sailing ship of a Christian type, whose sail bears the arms of ancient Portugal."[212]

While previous ceramics objects cited in this chapter have been most likely to have been produced in Málaga, the *Bowl* in figure 9 has been definitively identified. As Rosser-Owen explains, this bowl was classified as having been made in Valencia until 1983 when "analyses conducted on it…identified the provenance of schist inclusions in the clay body as the Málaga region."[213]

Speculative Analysis

Given the specific details of the ship depicted, Rosser-Owen contends it may be that this bowl was commissioned and produced for export: "The depiction of ships has a long tradition in the pottery of the Islamic west, but the type of ship which fills the

---

[212] Rosser-Owen, "Bowl: Historical Context."
[213] Rosser-Owen, "Bowl: Historical Context."

cavetto of this bowl is Christian. Its sail bears the arms of ancient Portugal, suggesting that it was commissioned by a Portuguese maritime merchant who wanted to commemorate his success through the ownership of a spectacular and expensive Málagan lustre bowl."[214]

The scientific proof that this "spectacular" bowl hails from Málaga and its Muslim artisans has anchored a better scholarly understanding of the importance of this city in the creation and promulgation of luster glazed ceramics—not only in late Medieval Islamic Iberia but throughout the Mediterranean region. Rosser-Owen underscores that "[t]hese results have been crucial for recognising the importance of the city's lustre industry… it is now generally agreed that the lustre technique was introduced to Valencia by potters from Málaga."[215] Further, she notes that by the start of the fifteenth century, "Valencia was rapidly overtaking Málaga as a supplier of fine pottery to the wealthy; and, though Málaga was not captured by the Catholic Kings until 1487, production there appears to have ceased abruptly" before the middle of the fifteenth century. Therefore, this particular bowl represents "the last great product of the Málaga lustre industry, made shortly before it disappeared."[216]

Conclusions

The most prolific production center of luster glazed ceramics on the Iberian Peninsula emerged in Málaga, a port city on the southern coast of the Islamic ruled Kingdom of Granada. Even though Islamic rulers had lost control of more than two thirds of the initial territory of *Al-Andalus*, Prince Ibn Ahmar was able to unify and establish the Nasrid Dynasty. Málaga emerged as this region's vital economic, artistic,

---

[214] Rosser-Owen, "Bowl: Historical Context."
[215] Rosser-Owen, "Bowl: Historical Context."
[216] Rosser-Owen, "Bowl: Historical Context."

and cultural hub despite the continuing onslaught and warfare of Christian rulers from northern Iberia trying to "re-conquer" the Kingdom of Granada. Málaga was highly fortified and in this highly embattled environment, traditional Islamic arts flourished.

As Málaga was connected to shipping routes throughout the Mediterranean basin, it was easy for Muslim artisans to immigrate here and for the import of required materials for their craft. Other elements contributing to Málaga's success in producing high quality luster glazed ceramics include preexisting infrastructure for ceramic production and several influxes of Muslim artisans felling political upheaval in Egypt and Persia.

Focusing on three of the Alhambra Vases created in Málaga provides insight into monumental technical and aesthetic achievements of Muslim artisans' mastery of the luster glaze ceramic forms and traditional Islamic decorative elements. The first vase displays a bold calligraphic message equating the power of Muslim rulers to the Divine power of God: the inscription refers in Arabic to kingship or dominion and is a contraction of a longer phrase meaning 'Power is with God.' The second vase displays the 'sacred hand' image which suggests an interrelationship between God's power and the King's power. The third vase though it is the most damaged contains an intact poem inscribed in calligraphy which addresses the "onlooker" inviting more personal contemplation than the messages on the prior vases.

The next two dishes use decorative schemes combining traditional Islamic motifs with Christian motifs while adding figurative imagery. The first dish may or may not be a Christian image. It shows a figure on horseback about to spear a giant serpent and, as such has been assumed to be a Christian image of St. George and the Dragon; however, both Muslims and Christians revere St. George. The second dish depicts a specific kind of Portuguese ship displaying a cross on its main sail—thus it is a Christian ship most likely commissioned by a Portuguese maritime merchant. This last dish, created just before the Christian re-conquest of Málaga, represents 'the last great product' of its luster glazed ceramics industry.

Chapter Three

Valencia's Emergence as an Economic, Artistic, and Cultural Center

This chapter investigates another center of production of Iberian luster glazed ceramics in a Christian ruled Kingdom of Aragon. Valencia, a central eastern coastal port, returned to Christian rule in 1238 after being a part of Islamic conquest in 711. By 1251, King James I of Aragon established religious tolerance based on the system used by Islamic Iberian rulers. According to Husband, the king "granted to all master artisans, regardless of religion, the right to work freely in several towns in the vicinity of Valencia upon payment of a small annual tax and a fee for each kiln."[217] Simultaneously, while conflict was increasing in Málaga it had decreased in Valencia where religious wars between Christians and Muslims had subsided. Given this environment of toleration and peace, an environment of cultural exchange flourished for almost three centuries in Valencia.

The port of Valencia (and nearby towns of Paterna, Mislata, and Manises clustered along the clay rich banks of the Turia River) faces east toward the Mediterranean Sea with easy access to European trading partners located in the ports of Marseilles, France and Genoa, Italy. Husband describes the geographic positioning, combined with the political climate, "must have been conducive to artistic production" because "artisans from Murcia and Málaga are known to have moved to the region of Valencia, where vast merchant fleets could ship their products unhindered."[218] The

---

[217] Husband, "Valencian Lusterware," 12-13.
[218] Husband, "Valencian Lusterware," 12-13.

Map 7. *Kingdoms of the Iberian Peninsula during the fourteenth and fifteenth centuries highlighting Valencia and environs.*

political climate at the port of Christian ruled Valencia was a vast improvement from what Rosser-Owen describes as blockades of 'Christian navies' interfering with export trade from Islamic-ruled Málaga; this was a definite impetus for some Muslim craftsmen to move north to settle nearby. In addition, she notes "[t]he rich clay-beds of the River Turia had supplied Valencian potters for centuries with the raw materials for a range of ceramics. The main centres of production were at Paterna and Manises, situated on opposite sides of the river."[219]

---

[219] Rosser-Owen, "Bowl: Historical Context."

At first, pottery producers in Valencia did not try to distinguish their work from the traditional Islamic decorative motifs and designs of luster glazed ceramics from Málaga. Muslim artisans in Valencia promoted themselves as 'masters of Málaga' and referred to their own ceramic ware production as *'obra de Malica'* (Málaga work). Husband explains: "Many Valencian documents refer to *'obra de Malica'* (work of Málaga), confirming the close association of that southern center with the region of Valencia—indeed, the term eventually became synonymous with Valencian lusterware. In one document, two Muslim potters are referred to as 'masters of Málaga, living in Manises.'"[220] Husband then confirms that 'Málagan expertise' referred not only to the shapes and forms but specifically to the special luster glazed ceramics: "The *'obra de Malica* of Manises is assumed to refer to lusterware because in a 1414 document that refers to *operis terre de Manises*, the last word has been erased and replaced with the term *Malica dauratum* (golden Málaga). Another record states that *obra de Malica* was gold lustered."[221]

Valencia by the fifteenth century became the largest production center of luster glazed ceramics in Iberia, eventually surpassing Málaga. Manises appears to have been the most prolific of the Valencia region production centers with the greatest number of surviving lusterware ceramics having originated from there. The quantity of production was driven by intense demand for Valencian wares, as Husband explains: "For an entire century, the lusterware industry of Valencia flourished. The pottery produced there, with its warm colors, its rich, metallic luster sheens so successfully imitating the patina of precious metals, and its pleasant designs intermingling Muslim and Christian motifs with

---

[220] Husband, "Valencian Lusterware," 12-13.
[221] Husband, "Valencian Lusterware," 12-13.

balance and grace, was certainly the finest available in Europe. Innumerable members of royal and noble houses in Spain, France, and Italy commissioned lusterware for both table service and decoration and had it emblazoned with their coats of arms."

As a testimony to Valencia's reputation for quality luster glazed ceramics by the start of the fifteenth century, Rosser-Owen notes that "Valencia was rapidly overtaking Málaga as a supplier of fine pottery to the wealthy."[222] Osma y Scull quotes Franciscan Friar Franscec Eiximenes, who in his 1383 work on civic duties, praised "the beauty of golden Manises wares, masterfully painted …[P]opes and cardinals and princes of the world seek it specially and are amazed that such an excellent and noble work can be made from earth."[223]

The toll of the ongoing religious wars between Muslims and Christians in Málaga was a dramatic decline in the number of Muslim artisans and thus a decline in the quantity of luster glazed ceramics produced there. In contrast, in Christian-ruled Valencia, religious wars between Christians and Muslims had subsided. Simultaneously, while conflict was increasing in Malaga it had decreased in Valencia. Therefore Valencia overtook and surpassed Málaga in production of luster glazed ceramics by both Muslim and Christian artisans.

Muslim, Múdejar, Mozarab, Christian, and Jewish Artisans

The immigration of skilled potters to the Valencia area had been going on prior since the mid-thirteenth century when, according to Nielson, Muslim artisans "migrated from Andalucia to the prosperous Christian kingdoms in the north of Spain, particularly

---

[222] Rosser-Owen, "Bowl: Historical Context."
[223] Guillermo Joaquin de Osma y Scull, *Apuntes Sobre Ceramica Morisca: Texto y Documentos Valencianos* (Madrid: M.G. Hernandez and Sons, 1906), 12, https://babel.hathitrust.org/cgi/pt?id=mdp.39015080256103;view=1up;seq=13.

to the town of Manises, near the port of Valencia. There they plied their trade, creating a golden pottery that was striking in appearance and prized both for its opulent elegance and practical utility."[224] Rosser-Owen summarizes, "it is now generally agreed that the lustre technique was introduced to Valencia by potters from Málaga."[225]

Many Muslim craftsmen who immigrated to Valencia and then converted to Christianity became known as *Múdejar*, as mentioned earlier. Similarly, Christians who had adapted to Islamic culture and adopted the Muslim style of dress and the Arabic language became known as *Mozarabs*. Thus, Husband asserts, "Muslims, Múdejares… and Christians were all working side by side."[226] It may be that there were some Jewish artisans in the workshops as well; recent documentation has confirmed the evidence of "Jews not as marginalized, passive victims, but as active protagonists in a cultural apparatus that was a great deal less segregated than was previously thought, working in studios composed of Christian, *Conversos* (Jews who converted to Christianity), and Jewish artists, who could turn out a Haggadah just as readily as they could a Catholic altarpiece."[227] The possibility of Jewish artisans participating in the creation of luster glazed ceramics will be addressed later in this chapter.

Though ceramic pieces examined in this dissertation are anonymous, many ceramic artisans of this time period are known by name due to the existence of contracts for leases of worksites, kilns, and work orders for commissions. Some ceramicist's work was so renowned, that, according to Husband, they were hired to travel throughout Spain

---

[224] Nielsen, *Devotion and Splendor*, 26.
[225] Rosser-Owen, "Bowl: Historical Context."
[226] Husband, "Valencian Lusterware," 12-13.
[227] Robin Cembalest, "The Torah in the Altarpiece," *Tablet Magazine* (2010), accessed March 18, 2016, http://www.tabletmag.com/jewish-arts-and-culture/25869/intermural-cooperation

and France to create tile work on site in the residences of nobility and even for the Pope.[228]

In addition, notes Husband, other artisans replicated luster glazed ceramics in their work: "Artists of the period, fascinated by its handsome designs and rich surface qualities, often depicted lusterware in the details of their panel painting and manuscript illumination."[229] Notable among these depictions is a predella, or shelf, from an altar in a Catholic church.

Figure 11. *The Last Supper*

Created in the early fifteenth century, the painting of *The Last Supper* in figure 11 is attributed to either Jaume Ferrer, the Elder, or Pere Teixidor. Painted in tempera on wood a part of an altarpiece at the church of Santa Constança in Linya, it measures 107 centimeters wide and 36 centimeters high. It is currently on display at the Regional Diocesan Museum of Solsona in northeastern Spain.[230] Museum curatorial notes pinpoint

---

[228] [B]y 1362, two such artisans, Juan Albalat and Pascasio Martin were well enough known to be summoned by Pope Aubert Audoin to Avignon to manufacture tiles for the palace... The career of Juan Murci is known in more detail. He began manufacturing tiles for the palace at Valencia in 1429. In 1444 he was contracted by Don Galceran de Requesens, who later became lieutenant general of Catalonia while Alfonso V was in Naples, to produce a rush order of nearly five thousand tiles. He was later commanded by Alfonso V to start tile pavements for the Castle of Gaeta and Castel Nuovo in Naples. By the time of his death in 1458, he was filling orders simultaneously for the castles at Naples and Valencia for over two hundred thousand tiles.

Valencian craftsmen are also known to have traveled within Spain to employ their art. In 1405, Muhammad Sulaiman al-Faki and Maymo Annajar, two master potters from Manises, which had become the major center of production, traveled to the province of Alicante where they remained for five years producing luster pottery.

The widespread fame of Valencian potters during the latter half of the fourteenth century is further substantiated by the inventories of the Duke of Berry. From them we know that a certain Jehan de Valence was commissioned by the Duke, between 1384 and 1386, to manufacture tiles for pavements in some of the apartments in the *tour de Maubergeon* at Poitiers. The tiles were described as white, green, and gold, and charged with the Duke's arms and motto. Jehan, well paid for his services, was allowed a staff of three assistants, one painter called Maître Richard, and six additional helpers.
Husband, "Valencian Lusterware," 12-13.

[229] Husband, "Valencian Lusterware," 12-13.

[230] Solsona, Spain is over 200 miles north of Valencia.

Figure 11. *The Last Supper,* by Jaume Ferrer the Elder or Pere Teixidor, early fifteenth century, tempera on wood, 107 x 36 cm. Originally from the church of Santa Constança in Linya; currently in Regional Diocesan Museum of Solsona, Solsona

Figure 12. *The Last Supper:* **Details**

"[t]he most striking detail in this version of the Last Supper is the tableware, especially the dishes, which are copies of the *Ave Maria* series that was produced by the famous pottery of Manises, which was active at the time this piece was painted."[231] (The *Ave Maria* series will be discussed later in fig. 25.) Sandra Curley in a Masters in Arts in History Thesis confirms the identification of the luster ceramics depicted in this painting

---

[231] "Last Supper, Church of Santa Constança," accessed August 5, 2016, http://visitmuseum.gencat.cat/en/museu-diocesa-i-comarcal-de-solsona/object/sant-sopar-de-l-esglesia-de-santa-constanca-de-linya/.

of *The Last Supper* stating that it "includes a detailed depiction of lusterware from Manises decorated with the Angelic Salutation, 'AVE MA/RIA GRA[CIA] PLE/NA,' around the rim." Further she adds, "[t]hese dishes combined the traditional Múdejar ornamentation with a gothic inscription of the Hail Mary for Christian patrons."[232]

Demand for luxurious luster glazed ceramics appeared to increase during the fifteenth century as those who could display their wealth were drawn to what may have seemed the more "affordable" form of metallic luster ceramics in light of shortages of more expensive precious metals according to Nielson: "Large dishes…were used for carrying food during feasts but also served as impressive decorative objects when displayed on sideboards. Their glittering appearance appealed to aristocratic users during the fifteenth century, when gold was in short supply."[233]

Replicating Traditional Islamic Motifs

As referred to earlier, there was great aesthetic value within Islamic cultures for decorative motifs replete with intricate ornamentation. A distinctive quality of much Islamic art is the use of patterns of decoration on all surfaces—whether on small objects or large architectural spaces: every surface provides the opportunity for ornamentation. These intricate designs could reflect combinations of motifs from the natural world, geometrically ordered shapes, and calligraphic inscriptions in Arabic which formed a coherent message, a reflection of *Allah* in all things. The decorative patterns employed are not arbitrary but rather are often intricate and interlocking systems of motifs employed to inspire devotion and reflection upon the vastness of the divine.

---

[232] Sandra Curley, "'Altogether Un-European:' Morisco Decorative Art and Spain's Hybrid Culture, 1492-1614," (Master's Thesis, Saint Mary's University, Halifax, Nova Scotia, 2014), 79-80.
[233] Nielsen, *Devotion and Splendor,* 26.

Figure13. *Bowl with Fatima's Hand and Paradise Keys*

At first *Bowl with Fatima's Hand and Paradise Keys* in figure13 may appear to be quite anomalous to ornate decorative schemes associated with traditional Islamic motifs.

Descriptive Analysis

Bowl with Fatima's Hand and Paradise Keys, created sometime in the fourteenth or fifteenth centuries measuring a width of 12.5 centimeters and a height of 7.3 centimeters,[234] resides at the González Martí National Museum of Ceramic and Sumptuary Arts in Valencia. A color scheme comprised of two hues: dark cobalt blue and a lustrous gold. Wear over time appears to have scraped some glaze off revealing some of the reddish earthenware hue visible to contemporary viewers. Decorative elements include: (1) Geometric elements; and (2) Figurative elements.

Perhaps most striking in the composition is the large area of uninterrupted reflective golden luster glaze and the lack of small decorative patterning in the background. The geometric shapes are evident in the straight lines of the keys, the arabesque curls, and a diamond shape as a part of the central image. Two keys flank the hand on either side their heads each a pointed arch shape; each key as a long shaft and appears to be standing upright on their notched tip—appearing like spears with pennants at their bases. Simple lines A delineate the figurative motif: a hand with fingers upraised fills the center of the bowl. Three curling arabesques on each side of the 'wrist' form the only decorative embellishment.

---

[234] Or, a width of almost 5 inches wide and a height of almost 3 inches.

Figure 13. *Bowl with Fatima's Hand and Paradise Keys.* Possibly Manises or Paterna, fourteenth-fifteenth centuries, width: 12.5 cm, height: 7.3 cm. González Martí National Museum of Ceramic and Sumptuary Arts, Valencia

Deductive Analysis

The so-called 'Fatima's Hand' refers to the Prophet Muhammad's daughter and is also called a 'sacred hand' or *hamsa*. According to Mari Paz Soler, Curator at González Martí National Museum of Ceramic and Sumptuary Arts, this 'Fatima's Hand' motif was popular not only with Muslim artisans but with *múdejar* craftsmen: "La hamsa es un tema recurrente en la decoración cerámica de la época islámica y posteriormente de la mudéjar."[235] As mentioned when discussing *Alhambra Vase (2)* (also known as the 'Hermitage Vase'), the *hamsa* resembles how Allah is written in Arabic. The decoration on this bowl is pared down from the elaborate systems of patterning evident on *Alhambra Vase (2)*.

The notable difference of this object from prior wares examined is its size—this bowl is relatively small—less than a third the size of most of the dishes (whether they be bowls, plates or platters) discussed in this dissertation; this bowl would easily fit in an individual's cupped hands. In addition, it stands out for the sheer simplicity of its decoration.

Speculative Analysis

The intent of the 'line drawing' for the hand may be to imitate Arabic script more closely than a drawing that appeared more like the stylized hand on *Alhambra Vase (2)*. Or perhaps utilizing five simple lines to render the hand could have been done to stress the numerical significance of the five fingers. Five is a significant number in Islam as the fundamental tenets are summed up as the 'Five Pillars of Islam.'[236] Perhaps for Muslims, the five fingers could serve as a reminder or a visual mnemonic device of the Five Pillars.

The 'Keys of Paradise' which flank the hand are symbols used more frequently in Christianity, according to Paz Soler. In a Christian context, the keys refer to the Kingdom of Heaven or to the Pope as the leader of the Catholic Church. Paz Soler

---

[235] Author's translation: "The *hamsa* is a recurring theme in the pottery of the Islamic period and later the múdejar decoration." Mari Paz Soler, "Bowl with Fatima's Hand and Paradise Keys: Classification," González Martí National Museum of Ceramic and Sumptuary Arts, accessed March 4, 2016, http://ceres.mcu.es/pages/Main?idt=12163&inventary=CE1/00747&table=FMUS&museum=MNC.

[236] The five pillars of Islam: profess faith, observe ritual prayer, give alms to the poor, fast during the month of Ramadan, and perform a pilgrimage to Mecca. "Five Pillars of Islam," accessed August 5, 2016, http://www.bbc.co.uk/religion/religions/islam/practices/fivepillars.shtml.

describes the history of the symbolism of "keys of paradise' within both Christian and Islamic art: "Las llaves del Paraíso que aparecen flanqueando la mano son también símbolos muy antiguos y por descontado apropiados para el cristianismo, con la simbología de las llaves del Reino o de la Iglesia. En el arte islámico se interpretan como las de la puerta del paraíso musulmán, y son mucho menos frecuentes que la hamsa."[237] Given that, as Paz Soler states, keys of Paradise are less frequently used by Muslim artisans, their use on this dish may suggest an intentional combination of faith references; that is, the pairing of the 'Hand of Fatima' (a Muslim reference) with the keys to the Kingdom of Heaven (a Christian reference) may reflect a *mudéjar* motif—one that combines Muslim and Christian identities.

The combination of Muslim decorative schemes used in the Christian-ruled region of Valencia with *mudéjar, mozarab, converso* and Jews, makes for multiple potential interpretations. Paz Soler notes the difficulty of comprehending the intent of the artisans: "Aunque esta escudilla tiene claros símbolos islámicos, no quiere decir eso que no fuera hecho para un ámbito cristiano, porque como hemos visto…el arte mudéjar incorpora plenamente esta simbología."[238]

Evidence of artisans or patrons who created or commissioned *Bowl with Fatima's Hand and Paradise Keys* does not exist nor does knowledge of who the intended audience was for viewing it. The intimate size of this bowl with simple decorations may mean the intended use was for personal reflection; in addition, the lack of pre-made holes

---

[237] Author's translation: "The keys of paradise which appear flanking the hand are also very old and of course appropriate symbols for Christianity, with the symbolism of the keys of the Kingdom (Heaven) or of the church. In Islamic art they are interpreted as (keys) of the Muslim gate of paradise, and are much less frequent(ly used) than the hamsa." Soler, "Bowl with Fatima's Hand: Classification."

[238] Author's translation: "Although this bowl has clear Islamic symbols, one cannot say that that was not done for a Christian context, because as we have seen …*mudéjar* art fully incorporates this (Christian) symbolism." Soler, "Bowl with Fatima's Hand: Classification."

in the rim could reinforce the interpretation that this bowl was intended for personal use rather than for wall display. This bowl contrasts starkly with the large scale luster glazed *Alhambra Vase (2)* which also utilizes the *hamsa* symbol but on a much more monumental scale intended to promote public reflection in the sumptuous surroundings of the Alhambra Palace.

Figure14. *Lustreware Basin*

More traditional Islamic decorative motifs appear on the *Lustreware Basin* in figure14 –a prototypical example of ceramic ware produced in Manises.

Descriptive Analysis

Lustreware Basin created in Manises between 1376 and 1425, measures a width of 38 centimeters and height of 5.5 centimeters[239] and is on display at the González Martí National Museum of Ceramic and Sumptuary Arts in Valencia. Upon close inspection, damage is evident in a series of cracks on the face of the dish. The color scheme utilizes three hues: a creamy white, cobalt blue, and a light gold luster glaze. Decorative elements include: (1) Floral and vegetative motifs; and (2) Geometric symbols.

The most visible floral motif appears in cobalt blue flowers framing the basin's inner rim. Clusters comprised of three flowers emanate from four points of the central image. Vegetative images such as leaves and vines are rendered in light gold luster on the white background surrounding the bold blue flowers as well as twining around the inner rim. Geometric shapes emanate from the central shape visually similar to the eight sided cobalt blue encircle the outer and inner rims. Undulating cobalt blue arabesques reminiscent of waves fill most of the width of the outer rim. Numerous other small

---

[239] Or, almost fifteen inches wide by just over 2 inches high.

Figure 14. *Lustreware Basin.* Manises, 1376 – 1425, width: 38 cm, height: 5.5 cm. González Martí National Museum of Ceramic and Sumptuary Arts, Valencia

geometric patterns, such as swirls, lines and cross hatching, all rendered in light gold luster on the white background fill every space between the arabesques.

Deductive Analysis

When viewed closely, there are two holes piercing the top rim (just above the largest curve form). When not in use, this kind of basin might be stored in a cupboard vertically to display the beauty of this prestigious object. While produced in Manises, this basin pays direct homage to traditional patterning originating in Málaga, adhering closely to the ornamentation and style of traditional Islamic motifs. This replication of and allegiance to Muslim craftsmanship is referred by the González Martí National Museum of Ceramic and Sumptuary Arts in Valencia with the somewhat archaic term "Muhammadan style decoration." [240]

Speculative Analysis

Given the ability for scientific testing that was able to attribute the *Bowl* in figure 9 to Malaga, it could be of interest to confirm the composition of the clay in this piece which seems so traditionally Islamic in its decorative motifs.

Figure 15. *Deep Dish*

The following *Deep Dish* in figure 15 bears a strong resemblance to the prior work, it shows innovations as well.

Descriptive Analysis

Deep Dish created circa 1430 measures a width of 45.1 centimeters and a height of 6 centimeters[241] and is on display in Gallery 10 at The Cloisters Collection of the Metropolitan Museum in New York City. The color scheme includes three hues: a creamy white, a deep cobalt blue, and an almost copper toned luster glaze. Decorative elements include: (1) Vegetative motifs; (2) Geometric symbols; and (3) Calligraphic inscriptions in Arabic.

The most visible vegetative motif rises in the shape of a deep cobalt blue stylized palm tree in the center of the dish with two lozenge shaped leaf forms on either side. The next band contains four more leaf forms which serve to separate calligraphic script. All

---

[240] "Lustreware Basin: Description," Museo Nacional de Ceramica y Artes suntuarias Gonzalez Marti de Valencia, accessed on February 5, 2016,
http://ceres.mcu.es/pages/Main?idt=31287&inventary=CE1/16800&table=FMUS&museum=MN

[241] Or, almost 18 inches wide and just over 2 inches high.

Figure 15. *Deep Dish.* Probably Manises, c. 1430, width: 45.1 cm, height: 6 cm. The Cloisters Collection—Metropolitan Museum, New York City

of the background motifs appear to be geometric on this piece. Four thin concentric bands of gold and cobalt blue encircle the outer and inner rims. The decorative style used around the rim replicates the arabesque waves rendered in cobalt blue as on the previous object—though the curves are more tightly rendered and compact, creating more of a sense of undulation. Again, replicating the prior piece, numerous geometric patterns, such as swirls, lines, and cross hatching, all rendered in the copper toned luster on the white background, fill every space between the arabesques. On this object these geometric patterns are more visible and create even more of a sense of movement as a result.

Deductive Analysis

According to curatorial notes at Metropolitan Museum, *Kufic* calligraphic script inscribed outside the central palm tree repeats an "*al-afiya* motif—a stylized shorthand of the Arabic word for 'health' and 'happiness.'"[242] At the top edge of the rim two holes were bored into the dish during its leather hard stage (prior to having been glazed) which would allow for it both display and contemplation of its messages.

Speculative Analysis

This capacious dish may have been made for a Muslim patron as it has with its legible Kufic script; this cannot be definitively proven as noted earlier, Menocal stated there were many Christian *Mozarabs* who "were so 'Arabized' that they "had to have their Bibles translated into Arabic."[243]

The combination of stylistic elements is consistent with the traditional Islamic motifs initiated in Malaga which appear to be faithfully adhered to in this piece. And curators identify this as "probably" hailing from Manises, as with the prior object, given the ability for scientific testing to determine the composition of the clay, it could be of interest to confirm the origin of this dish definitively.

Figure 16. *Plate*

On the *Plate* in figure 16 similar motifs from the prior dish combine with new elements.

---

[242] "Deep Dish: Notes," Metropolitan Museum, accessed December 28, 2015, http://www.metmuseum.org/art/collection/search/471813?rpp=60&pg=1&ft=ceramics%2bspain&pos=50

[243] Menocal, "Visions," 13.

Descriptive Analysis

Plate created in the late fourteenth to early fifteenth centuries measuring a width of 44.9 centimeters and a height of 7 centimeters is in The Cloisters Collection of the Metropolitan Museum of Art in New York City. There is one visible chip out of the upper right rim. The color scheme echoes almost exactly the prior object and includes three hues: a creamy white, a deep cobalt blue, and a copper toned luster glaze. Decorative elements include: (1) Floral and vegetative motifs; (2) Geometric symbols; and (3) Calligraphic inscriptions in Arabic.

The floral and vegetative motifs include a flower with twelve petals painted loosely in white at the core then outlined by dark blue interlocking petal forms. Four palm trees emanate from the geometric star shape in the center of the plate with tree tops stretching to the plate's outer rim. Each palm tree is flanked by a pair of small copper medallion shapes with what appear to be stylized flowers.

The central floral motif is encased in a series of geometric motifs. An eight pointed star comprised of two interlocking squares echoes the star on *Alhambra Vase (3)*. Within the star, blue and gold hues delineate an octagon. Replicating the prior piece, numerous geometric patterns, including a preponderance of swirls, lines, and wavy lines, all rendered in the copper toned luster on the white background, fill every available space.

Deductive Analysis

While this plate, with its intricate ornamentation, is clearly intended for decorative as well as functional use, the position of the two holes incised in the plate's edge are in a location that would not allow it to be hung in a symmetrical

Figure 16. *Plate.* Probably Manises, late fourteenth - early fifteenth centuries, width: 44.9 cm, height: 7 cm. The Cloisters Collection—Metropolitan Museum of Art, New York City

fashion; the holes are currently visible in the upper left edge (at roughly ten o'clock if it were a clock face). Curators at the Metropolitan Museum describe the calligraphic inscriptions as connected to *Kufic* style script. They are not translated so they may not be legible or may be the beginning of what becomes termed "pseudo

Kufic script" when artisans would mimic the shape of Arabic script without actually writing legible words.[244]

Speculative Analysis

Again, the motifs combined on this object replicate traditional Islamic motifs initiated in Malaga—though the less legible script hints of deviations. As curators list this as "probably" created in Manises, as with the prior object, given the ability for scientific testing to determine the composition of the clay, it could be of interest to confirm the origin of this dish definitively. It may be a sign of the demands of mass production that the holes were bored into the leather hard clay before the design was adhered and the artisan did not line up the plate before painting on the glaze patterns.

When looked at from a distance, the largest motifs on the plate, the four palm trees and the four strips of pseudo Kufic script, each appear as equidistant crosses creating an intriguing image of two intersecting crosses. Thus while the visual components—the palm trees and apparent Arabic script—remain identifiably Islamic in origin, their composition may show Christian influences.

Christian Family Coats of Arms Motifs

The largest quantity of surviving luster glazed ceramics from the Iberian Peninsula are the fifteenth century dishes produced in and around Valencia which feature family coats of arms for nobility throughout Europe, according to Neilson and Rosser-Owen. The turning point seems to have been the start of the fifteenth century; Rosser-Owen explains that in Manises "after 1400 the kilns produced superb lustreware, ceramics with an overglaze painting in lustre, which gives pieces a distinctive metallic

---

[244] "Plate: Note," Metropolitan Museum, http://www.metmuseum.org/collection/the-collection-online/search/468520

sheen. These pieces were often decorated with armorial designs for Spanish and Italian customers."[245] Neilson describes these pieces as follows: "The most common motif on Hispano-Moresque pottery is a Christian coat of arms surrounded by Moorish ornament...[S]uch items were often ordered to commemorate marriages."[246] According to Ray, in fifteenth century Valencia "new 'Christian' motifs were incorporated into the decorative repertoire in a cheaper more coppery luster on more simply potted forms."[247]

The following metallic luster glazed ceramic works chart the evolution of the designs for the heraldic family crests and newly developed production techniques.

Figure 17. *Plate with the Arms of Blanche of Navarre*

The first example of ceramic works with coats of arms, *Plate with the Arms of Blanche of Navarre* in figure 17, shows a commission for a Spanish Christian Queen.

Descriptive Analysis

Plate with the Arms of Blanche of Navarre, definitively created in Manises between1427 to 1438 and measuring a width of 40 centimeters,[248] resides in the Cloisters Collection of the Metropolitan Museum in New York City. Slight damage is evident on the rim where small portions are chipped revealing the underlying reddish brown earthenware clay. The color scheme contains three hues: opaque white, deep cobalt blue, and a lustrous gold. Decorative elements include: (1) Floral and vegetative motifs; (2) Geometric designs; and (3) Figurative elements.

The floral and vegetative elements fill the outer and inner rim with alternating deep cobalt blue and gold seven pointed leaves on a white background linked by gently

---

[245] Rosser-Owen, "Bowl: Historical Context."
[246] Nielsen, *Devotion and Splendor*, 25.
[247] Ray, *Spanish Pottery*, 137.
[248] Or, a width of almost 16 inches.

Figure 17. *Plate with the Arms of Blanche of Navarre.* Manises, 1427-38, width: 40 cm. The Cloisters Collection—Metropolitan Museum, New York City

undulating thin vines of blue and gold. Twining between these larger leaves are multiple golden shapes such as small flowers, small symmetrical fern fronds, and thin curling vines.

The coat of arms is the largest design element on the plate taking up almost half of the plate's surface. Geometric shapes comprise quadrant demarcations within the family crest. The upper left quadrant contains a series of gold orbs threaded on six spokes emanating from a central circle on a white background. The lower left quadrant shows five white *fleur de lys* shapes on a gold background. The right half is itself bisecting by an 'x' shape—in the top and bottom parts gold and white stripes appear in an almost hour glass shape.

Figurative elements appear on either side of the stripes: to the left, a three towered castle, and to the right, a griffin faces left as it rears on its back legs. Resting atop the coat of arms rests a crown; underneath the crown, dark golden cross-hatching beneath the bottom rounded edge of the crown and the coat of arms suggests a three dimensional view in which the family crest is 'wearing' the crown.

Deductive Analysis

This plate, as described by the Metropolitan Museum curator, "bears the prominent arms of Queen Blanche of Navarre (1391–1441) and her husband, John II of Aragon, was probably part of a larger service."[249] When comparing its shape and design to subsequent luster ceramic ware with coats of arms, it is evident this plate is an early example before standardization of bowls with wider rims and smaller coats of arms at the center (as will be seen in future examples).

Speculative Analysis

While the intent of those who commissioned the plate's design may have been to impress the viewer with royal power as conveyed by the coat of arms, the artisans choice of using the same golden hue to delineate the coat of arms, its crown, and so many of the surrounding leaf shapes reduces the contrast and flattens the image.

---

[249] "Plate with the Arms of Blanche of Navarre: Note," Metropolitan Museum, accessed December 19, 2016, http://www.metmuseum.org/collection/the-collection-online/search/471801.

This may been part of the artisan's intent: to show that the rulers are a part of the natural world or need to be connected to the natural order of things.

Figure 18. *Deep Dish*

Deep Dish in figure 18 shows the standardization of patterning used on the coat of arms luster ceramic ware.

Descriptive Analysis

Deep Dish, produced in Manises between 1430 and 1460 measuring a width of 47.6 centimeters, this object resides in the Cloisters Collection of the Metropolitan Museum in New York City. The color scheme consists of four hues: creamy white, deep cobalt blue, reddish-purple, and golden luster. Decorative elements include: (1) Floral and vegetative motifs; (2) Geometric designs; and (3) Figurative elements.

The floral and vegetative motifs cover roughly half of surface of the dish with clusters of precisely replicated dark blue flowers with six petals each and a gold circle at the center accompanied by dark blue tri-part leaves. Twined between these motifs are multiple thin gold curling vines. Arranged around the central circle an array of thirteen segments, each delineated by thin blue arching lines replicating the shape of a petal, contains a repeating pattern of five elements: three flowers and two leaves. At the center a wide band of cobalt blue circles the coat of arms. Twelve white vegetative images decorate this blue band; a central teardrop shape joins two interlocking "u" shapes with small white fringes above and below them.

Geometric motifs are implicit within the ordering of the floral and vegetative shapes. Additionally, there are several circle patterns from thin blue circles around

Figure 18. *Deep Dish.* Manises, 1430-1460, width: 47.6 cm. The Cloisters Collection—Metropolitan Museum, New York City

many of the flowers, to a thin blue interlocking rope pattern that outlines the central blue circle which frames the coat of arms.

The primary figurative element emerges on the coat of arms: an animal rendered in reddish-purple facing left and rearing up on its hind legs with its tail arching up to the right. The whites of its slanted eye and pointed fangs are visible. Its fur is etched in wavy white lines revealed through the *sgraffitto* technique. Anatomical details include its penis extending from its abdomen and four sharp claws extending from each of its paws. This fierce animal appears on an asymmetrical golden shield.

Deductive Analysis

Deep Dish was commissioned by delle Agli family of Florence, according to Metropolitan Museum curatorial notes, and it "comes from a lavish ensemble of tableware." The delle Agli "family's arms, featuring a rampant wolf, appears at the center." The wolf was supposed to be red but apparently the "purplish color is as close as the potters could get. to the prescribed red." The blue ring contains a ring of "garlic, a playful reference to the consonance between the family name and the Italian word for garlic *(aglio)*."[250]

The decorative floral and vegetative border covers a large portion of the dish creating a vibrant and dynamic scrolling vine pattern, which is identified in curatorial notes as bryony flowers.[251] This stylized manner of depicting the bryony pattern became the standard which is repeated in dozens (if not hundreds) of extant luster glazed luster ware pieces. It is perhaps the most distinctive decorative pattern from this era and, according to Caiger-Smith, appeared was a design in use as early as 1427.[252]

Speculative Analysis

This dish appears to exemplify the beginnings of standardized proportions for production of these increasing popular dishes: the coats of arms are rendered smaller and the surrounding edges and rims replete with intertwining flowers and leaves

---

[250] "Deep Dish: Note," Metropolitan Museum, accessed December 28, 2016, http://www.metmuseum.org/collection/the-collection-online/search/471805?rpp=30&pg=1&rndkey=20151123&ft=*&where=Manises&pos=5

[251] "Deep Dish: Note," Metropolitan Museum.

[252] Caiger-Smith, *Lustre Pottery,* 113.

occupy more space. Another process which may have been standardized on this plate was how the coat of arms was drawn; its smaller size of the crest (compared to the prior example) may have been precipitated by the large size of sets of dishware ordered—and it being easier to copy smaller images. Later pieces to be examined exhibit coats of arms that appear to be stenciled in order to provide consistency of the images from piece to piece.

Figure 19. *Dish*

In the following *Dish* in figure 19 similarities to the previous dish are evident as well as innovations.

Descriptive Analysis

Created in Manises between 1430 and 1470, this *Dish* measures a width of 44.6 centimeters,[253] and belongs to the collection of the Victoria and Albert Museum in London. Damage to this piece includes two chips where no glaze remains—one on the outer rim and one on the inner rim. The color scheme consists of three hues: creamy white, cobalt blue, and yellow-gold luster. Decorative elements include: (1) Floral and vegetative motifs; (2) Geometric motifs; (3) Calligraphic inscription in Latin; and (4) Figurative images.

The floral and vegetative elements dominate the decorative scheme of this dish. There appears to be equilibrium between the number of blue flowers and gold leaves as well as an even number of blue and gold tendrils and vines curling between spaces. Of note, at the juncture where the corners of coat of arms contact the inner circle thin blue stems radiate up and out in thin branches sketching out four loosely rendered bush shapes that fill the inner rim.

---

[253] Or, a width of roughly 17 ½ inches.

Figure 19. *Dish.* Manises, 1430-70, width: 44.6 cm. Victoria and Albert Museum, London

Geometric motifs include circles and squares. Concentric thin blue rope designs encircle the central coat of arms and the inner edge of the outer rim. Outlined by thin cobalt blue lines, four squares within a square structure the representation of the coat of arms.

Three words inscribed in cobalt blue Gothic style calligraphic script (similar to the style used in Christian illustrated manuscripts) ring the outer rim of the dish. The words appear evenly spaced with *"equi"* at the top center, *"noia"* on the lower right, and *"marya"* on the lower left.

Contained within the four squares of the family crest at the center of the dish are repeating figurative motifs rendered in gold on a white background. Enclosed in the upper left and lower right quadrants are three tiered towers while the upper right and lower left quadrants contain a bull facing left (three-quarter view).

Deductive Analysis

Described by Ray, the coat of arms on this dish proves its origin in Mansises as it is the family crest of "an unidentified member of the Buyl (or 'Boyl' or 'Boil') family" who became "Lords of Manises" allowing them "to control and encourage the pottery industry already established there."[254] The good condition of the glaze suggests this was a prized item—perhaps used infrequently or only for display. Of note, there are no holes in the outer rim (as several other pieces have had); by this time, wealthy families with prized decorative luster glazed ceramic dishes like this may have propped it up "with others like it on a stepped structure erected during grand meals to show off the host's fine dining pieces" according to Ray.[255]

The glazing pattern resembles the prior plate especially in its application of the color palette. However, though this dish also uses opaque white for the background decorated with blue and gold floral and vegetative patterns, it differs in several ways: (1) This dish contains an apparently lighter shade of cobalt blue for the bryony flowers; (2) More golden luster glaze is used on the numerous interstitial leaves and vines; and (3) Most noticeably, Gothic calligraphy appears on the broad rim. Gothic calligraphy is

---

[254] "Dish: Note," Victoria and Albert Museum, accessed December 28, 2016, http://collections.vam.ac.uk/item/O155420/dish-dish-unknown/

[255] "Dish: Note," Victoria and Albert Museum.

perhaps best known from Christian medieval illustrated manuscripts, and, as such, is definitely refers to European influences as opposed to the Arabic calligraphy found on earlier Muslim influenced luster glazed ceramics.

Speculative Analysis

The calligraphic script on this dish may reflect a Christian message. The three word inscription which decorates the outer rim reads: "equi noia marya." This phrase is translated, without derivation, by Rosser-Owen as "here [is the] girl mary."[256] The confusion may arise from an artisan's incorrect transcription of the phrase—that is, two incorrect letters. The language spoken in Valencia was Catalàn and in this language, "here girl mary" would be written "aquí noia maria."[257] If indeed the motto was intended to be understood as "here [is the] girl mary," then this script could be a reference to the young Virgin Mary.

The coat of arms, according to Ray, may be those of Pedro, fourth Lord of Manises, who died in 1454 noting the same arms (but with the quarters reversed) appear on two later dishes in the Cloisters Collection…and in the Musee de Lyon.[258] This dish "would have been produced in a workshop as part of a larger commission. This is not only suggested by the fact that other dishes with this design and motto survive…[but also because] the stenciled heraldic charges in the dish bowl also suggest these motifs had to be produced many times over."[259]

---

[256] Rosser-Owen also notes that Ray transcribes the message 'MARIA EQUI NOIA' and does not attempt to translate it. "Dish: Marks and Inscriptions," Victoria and Albert Museum, accessed December 28, 2016, http://collections.vam.ac.uk/item/O155420/dish-dish-unknown/.

[257] Catalan is "a romance language spoken in the regions of Catalan and Valencia with some commonalities with Spanish." "Catalan (català)," *Omniglot.com*, s.v. "Catalan (català)," the accessed August 5, 2016, http://www.omniglot.com/writing/catalan.htm. Translations from Catalan to English: http://www.bing.com/translator/?ref=TThis&text=&from=es&to=en

[258] Ray, *Spanish Pottery*, 121.

[259] "Dish: Note," Victoria and Albert Museum.

Patterns of Change: Four Examples of Changing Production Methods

Figure 20. *Plate*

Figure 21. *Dish with Heraldic Shield*

Figure 22. *Ewer Basin*

Figure 23. *Brasero Dish*

The following four dishes are included less for the specificity of the decoration or the particular family crests but more as an opportunity to show a pattern of evolution of the shapes and glazing patterns of these luxurious golden luster plates and dishes.

Descriptive Analysis

Both the *Plate* in figure 20 and *Dish with Heraldic Shield* figure 21 show the development of what may have been molds or perhaps stenciled overlays of 'slip' cords on the leather hard clay base to produce what appear as low relief petal forms which rise off the dish's surface. Notice that rather than creating a pattern of flowers on the background of the dish or around the rim, the object itself comes to resemble a large flower which the family crest accentuated in the center. On figure 21, not only are the 'ribs' of the petals articulated with this raised patterning, but they almost become three dimensional balls.

The *Ewer Basin* in figure 22 and the *Brasero Dish* in figure 23 represent the further development of the petal design with more tightly compact renderings of the petal forms. In figure 22 there are two layers: the first layer comprised of curved petals radiating out from the central coat of arms which features a griffin; and the second layer comprised of straight edged petals which line the outer rim. Figure 23 contains two

Figure 20. *Plate.* Manises, 1470-1490, width: 43.2 cm. The Cloisters Collection—Metropolitan Museum, New York City

Figure 21. *Dish with Heraldic Shield.* Manises, 1470-1500, width: 43.5 cm. Metropolitan Museum, New York City

Figure 22. *Ewer Basin.* Valencia, c. 1525-1575, 37 cm. The Walters Art Museum, Baltimore

Figure 23. *Brasero Dish.* Manises, late fifteenth-early sixteenth centuries, width: 49.1 cm. Metropolitan Museum, New York City

layers of petals as well with both of them curved. On this dish, between the layers of petals bands alternate between dot patterns and intricately detailed leaf and vine motifs.

Deductive Analysis

Of note, three of these forms (with the exception of "fig. 21") have a very high gloss metallic lustrous glaze which combined with some of the low relief forms may be in an effort to mimic metalwork of the time. *Brasero Dish* in figure 23 is emblematic of this style, according to Metropolitan Museum curatorial notes: "In the late 15th century a shift in the taste led to the production of this type of dish, called 'gadrooned ware.' Characterized by the raised and tapered gadroon[260] decoration around the outer rim and inner raised boss, this design was borrowed from contemporary metalwork, which often comprised raised decorative elements."[261] The decorative style of *Dish with Heraldic Shield* in figure 21 is related to metalwork as well as a plate with similar design is described as "'goldsmith style' with a decoration of painted 'striped seeds' and 'fine diaper of dots and stalks.'"[262]

Clearly, there was great demand for luster glazed ceramic dishes featuring coats of arms for Christian families. These ceramic objects were clearly highly prized within the families that commissioned them. That so many remain in excellent condition over five hundred years after their creation is a testimony to the esteem with which these lusterware ceramics were held.

Speculative Analysis

Changes in the production methods used for making these dishes featuring coats of arms were based on structural or formal elements—presumably to improve the speed

---

[260] Gadroon is defined as "a decorative edging on metal or wood, typically formed by inverted flutings." *OxfordDictionary.com*, s.v. "gadroon," accessed March 18, 2016, http://www.oxforddictionaries.com/us/definition/american_english/gadroon.

[261] "Brasero Dish: Note," Metropolitan Museum, accessed December 10, 2016, http://www.metmuseum.org/art/collection/search/451995?rpp=90&pg=1&ft=spain%2c+ceramics&pos=56.

[262] "Concave Lustreware Plate with Lion: Note," Google Arts & Culture, accessed December 10, 2016, https://www.google.com/culturalinstitute/beta/asset/concave-lustreware-plate-with-lion/fgGF0ic3a_1ORA.

with which artisans could produce these very popular objects. Perhaps the quantity of commissions or requests from patrons are what pushed the production centers to adapt the forms and styles used to decorate them.

Islamic and Christian Motifs

While the first examples of luster glazed ceramics examined at the start of this chapter maintained the traditional Islamic decorative motifs developed by Muslim craftsmen in Málaga, other decorative motifs evolved in the Valencia region. And as previous examples showed, many Christian patrons within Iberia and from afar commissioned ornately decorated luster glazed ceramics to prominently display their family coat of arms. Thus, the luster glazed ceramic ware began to reflect not only traditional Islamic motifs but also incorporate unambiguous motifs from other faiths such as Christianity and Judaism. The following four objects exemplify the combination—or *'convivencia'*— of Islamic and Christian motifs.

Figure 24. *Plate*

Incorporating Christian motifs, the *Plate* in figure 24 shows an example of luster glazed ceramic ware that became much sought after.

Descriptive Analysis

Created in Manises between 1430 and 1450, the *Plate* in figure 24 measures a width of 37.3 centimeters[263] and resides in the Cloisters Collections of the Metropolitan Museum in New York City. Slight damage is evident in two chips in the glaze on the lower right inner and outer rims. The color scheme includes three hues: creamy white, deep cobalt blue and lustrous copper. Decorative elements include: (1) Geometric

---

[263] Or, a width of just over 14 ½ inches.

Figure 24. *Plate.* Manises, 1430-1450, width: 37.3 cm. The Cloisters Collections—Metropolitan Museum, New York City

motifs; (2) Figurative representation of a dragon; and (3) Calligraphic inscription in Latin.

Geometric motifs appear on the creamy white background as several constellations of copper-toned luster circles and dots. Husband describes this design as "lustered discs, singly and in groups of threes and fours, entwined with semicircular loops on a diapered ground."[264] Three concentric circles mark the inner rim with two deep cobalt blue circles encasing a central lustrous copper band.

The central motif shows a figurative representation in deep cobalt blue of what the Cloisters Collection of the Metropolitan Museum entitles a "dragon." However, in purely graphic terms, this animal bears close resemblance to creatures called "serpents" on other luster glazed ceramics.[265] Instead of a coiled tail this dragon's tail is a short stub, and the fringed diagonal lines on its torso suggest wings. With its head reared back and mouth open wide displaying its outstretched curling tongue, this creature stands in profile facing left on two hind legs much like the wolf shown on a coat of arms dish earlier.[266]

The deep cobalt blue calligraphic inscription wraps around the plate's outer rim. The apparent Latin inscription rendered in six evenly spaced clusters of Gothic style calligraphy reads: '*ave ma ria, gra ple na.*'

Deductive Analysis

Luster ceramic wares with this style of Gothic Latin calligraphy inscription were popular and prevalent in this era as evidenced by the painting of *The Last Supper* in figure 11. The calligraphy appears to be a truncated version of the complete Biblical phrase which in Latin would read: '*Ave Maria, gra**tia** plena*'[267] (with the three missing letters in bold face)—the phrase used in the Annunciation of the Virgin Mary— the announcement made by angel to Mary by that she is pregnant with Jesus. This

---

[264] Husband, "Valencian Lusterware," 25.
[265] See figure 7, *Bowl with Horseman Spearing Serpent* and figure 26, *Dish*.
[266] See figure 18, *Deep Dish*.
[267] In Metropolitan Museum's bulletin there is no mention of the missing letters—instead, the author simply fills them in.

translates to 'Hail Mary, Full of Grace" the opening line of the 'Ave Maria' prayer, one of the most frequently recited prayers within the Catholic tradition.

Speculative Analysis

The missing letters could have happened because the artisan rendering the calligraphy was not actually conversant in Latin—but this is speculation as the artisan who created this plate is unknown. Nor is the name of the patron known—though it would seem to be made for a Christian audience.

The dragon in the center could be an evolution of the serpent. Daniel Ogden explains that the Christian tradition of saintly dragon slayers incorporates "an infusion of serpent symbolism" from the Hebrew and Christian Bibles.[268] With head reared back and mouth open wide, the dragon appears to be preparing for a fight or reeling from a blow. This posture could be explained by the message of the Annunciation which some would pair with a passage from Genesis 3:15 in the Hebrew Bible with God addressing the serpent in the Garden of Eden: "I will put enmity between you and the woman, and between your offspring and hers; he will strike your head, and you will strike his heel."[269]

Figure 25. *Dish*

The imagery on the *Dish* in Figure 25 is comparable to a bowl already examined in the Chapter 2, that is, the *Bowl with Horseman Spearing a Serpent* in figure 7.

Descriptive Analysis

This *Dish*, created circa 1450 and measuring a width of 45.4 centimeters,[270] resides in the Cloisters Collection of the Metropolitan Museum of Art in New York City.

---

[268] Daniel Ogden, *Dragons, Serpents, and Slayers in the Classical and Early Christian Worlds: A Sourcebook* (Oxford: Oxford University Press, 2013), 5.
[269] Gen. 3:15 (New Revised Standard Version).
[270] Or, almost 18 inches wide.

Figure 25. *Dish.* Probably Manises, c. 1450, width: 45.4 cm. The Cloisters Collection—Metropolitan Museum of Art, New York City

Three kinds of damage exist: (1) The golden luster glaze is quite worn, especially in the center of the dish, rendering some of the imagery less distinct; (2) A noticeable dark crack runs from the lower center of the inner ring to the outer rim at the bottom of the dish; and (3) Scattered throughout the surface are multiple black pock marks. The color scheme includes two hues: creamy white and golden luster; all decorations are inscribed in gold on the white background. Decorative elements include: (1) Floral and vegetative motifs; and (2) Figurative representations of a man and three animals.

Floral and vegetative motifs fill the entire surface of this dish with a combination of bryony flowers, multiple leaf shapes including ferns, and thin swirling vines. On the upper half of the bowl's rim three sets of large leaves with twined stems create a stylized wooded canopy.

Figurative representations include a rider, a horse, a deer, and a dragon. Horse and rider appear to be bounding just above the center point of the bowl. The entire scene on this *Dish* bursts out of the center circle onto the outer rim.[271] Depicted facing right, the rider's arms appear to be swinging out. His left hand clenches the reins and his left hand grasps a spear. Due to worn glaze and to the low contrast of using one golden hue to delineate all the shapes, it is difficult to locate the rider's spear; it is held in the bent back right arm of the rider positioned next to him and his horse with its tip poised in front of the mouth of the giant serpent. The rider seems to wear padded armor with textured wide sleeves and pants.

Of the three animals depicted, the horse takes up the most space. Shown in profile facing right, the striding horse raises its front hooves and lowers its head to confront the serpent by gazing directly into its eyes. The dish's most visible decoration appears on the horse's rear right flank: a large white equidistant cross with pointed ends. A small deer appears cowering in the foliage on the lower left side of the dish; lifting its head up diagonally to the left, the deer looks to the cross symbol emblazoned on the horse's flank. The serpent coiled in the lower right of the dish appears smaller than the

---

[271] The rider's head and elbow jut into the upper rim, the horse's hindquarters and tail jut onto the left rim, the legs and body of a cowering deer tuck into the lower left rim, and the serpent's curled tail, wing and head span the lower to right sides of the rim.

Figure 26. Comparison: (fig. 7) *Bowl with Horseman Spearing Serpent* & (fig. 25) *Dish*

horse and its position is submissive with its head lower than the horse's. This composition shows the moment the serpent is being pinned to the ground by the horse.

Deductive Analysis

This *Dish* evokes comparison with the *Bowl with a Horseman Spearing a Serpent* in figure 7. (See "fig. 26" for a side by side comparison.) Both objects are almost the same size (the *Bowl* is 44 centimeters and the *Dish* is 45.4 centimeters) and their compositions both depict the moment before a rider on horseback spears a huge coiled serpent. The most notable distinctions are: (1) The main figurative images of rider, horse and dragon appear facing in opposite directions in an almost mirror image; (2) The quality of craftsmanship, that is, the way that the figures are rendered, differs greatly with the draftsmanship on figure 25 appearing less precise; (3) The color schemes differ as well as the use of only two pale tones on figure 25 makes it literally pale in comparison to the strong clear tones used to delineate the scene on the *Bowl* in figure 7; and (4) Only the

Dish in figure 25 contains an overt Christian image with the equidistant white cross on the horse's rear flank.

This is one of the luster glazed pieces with pre-cut holes made visible above and to the right of the rider's head suggesting that part of its intended use was as an object of display.

Speculative Analysis

The image on this dish may be a reference to the Christian legend of Saint George and the dragon—or it could equally be a Muslim rendition of the same story as Hovannisian and Sabagh explain that "Saint George is something of an exception among saints and legends, in that he is known and revered by Muslims."[272]

Given the compositional similarities of this later Manises-made *Dish* with the earlier Málaga-made *Bowl with a Horseman Spearing a Serpent* it seems plausible that the artisan who created the later *Dish* was familiar with or could have intentionally tried to copy the earlier *Bowl*.

Figure 27. *Plate*.

An obvious Christian image appears prominently on the decorative scheme of the *Plate* in Figure 27—a pattern that was replicated often due to its popularity.

Descriptive Analysis

Created between 1430 and 1460, this *Plate*, measuring a width of 45.4 centimeters, resides in the Cloister Collection of the Metropolitan Museum in New York City. This object is in excellent condition with no visible signs of external damage. The color scheme consists of three hues: creamy white, deep cobalt blue, and lustrous copper.

---

[272] Hovannisian and Sabagh, *Religion and Culture in Medieval Islam*, 109-110.

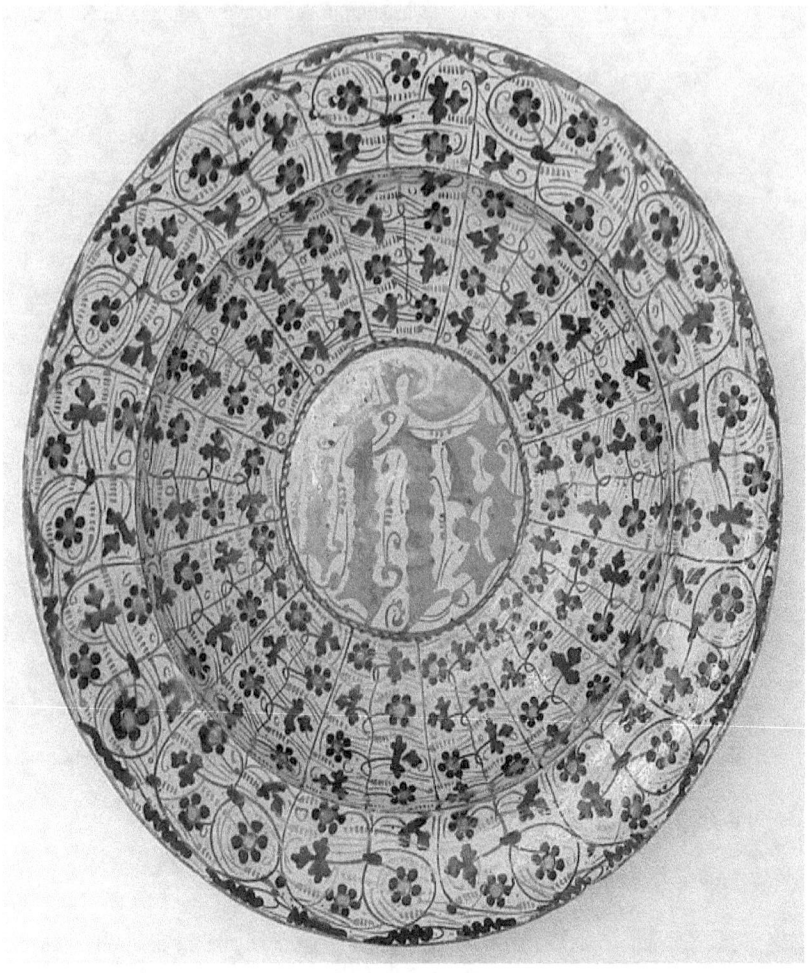

Figure 27. *Plate.* Probably Manises, c. 1430-1460, width: 45.4 cm. The Cloister Collection—Metropolitan Museum, New York City

Decorative elements include: (1) Floral and vegetative motifs; (2) Geometric motifs; and (3) Calligraphic inscription.

The floral and vegetative designs comprise over three quarters of the plate's surface area. The pattern of alternating bryony flowers and leaves, each rendered in the deep cobalt blue emanate from the central circle in thirteen petal shaped clusters delineated by thin blue lines; from the inner circle to the outer rim, four flowers and four leaves are paired while above the rim, curled within outer edge of the petal are three flowers and two leaves.[273] Thin lustrous copper vines and tendrils twine through the flowers and leaves as well as through the space surrounding the calligraphic letters in the center.

The only geometric element is a pair of interlocking thin cobalt blue lines framing the central circle with a rope pattern. Within this circle lies the central inscription: an 'IHS' monogram marked with opaque white for the background and a lustrous deep copper for the large letters. Each letter is made more dynamic in appearance by the use of wavy lines to construct them.

Deductive Analysis

Shown in Gothic style calligraphy, the central motif 'IHS' is a 'Christogram' (or 'monogram of Christ'). German semiotics historian Udo Becker explains, it represents "the first three letters of the Greek name of Jesus, IHΣOYΣ, *iota-eta-sigma*, or IHΣ…The Greek letter *iota* is represented by I, and the *eta* by H, while the Greek letter *sigma* is…represented by S."[274]

Speculative Analysis

This particular combination with an ornate 'IHS' inscribed in Gothic style calligraphy surrounded by rhythmic repetitions of the popular bryony flower, leaves and tendrils pattern may be one of the most popular styles of Valencian luster glazed ceramics. Numerous examples of almost exact repetitions of this desing have survived and are on display in multiple locations. Of the four at The Cloister Collection of the

---

[273] See figure 18, *Deep Dish* for a similar clustering and ordering of the bryony flower pattern.
[274] Udo Becker, *The Continuum Encyclopedia of Symbols* (London: Continuum Publishing, 2000), 54.

Metropolitan Museum this *Plate* is distinguished from the other three by its accession number: 56.171.143. Some of the other known examples are two at the Hispanic Society of America in New York, one at the Cluny Museum in Paris, and one at the Burrell Collection in Glasgow, Scotland.

Figure 28. *Deep Dish*.

Exemplifying evolution and change in the decorative motifs of Valencia, the *Deep Dish* in figure 28 shows many innovations.

Descriptive Analysis

Created in Manises circa 1440, this *Deep Dish* measures a width of 47.2 centimeters and a depth of 13.4 centimeters[275] and is on display in Gallery 16 in The Cloisters Collection of the Metropolitan Museum in New York City. This dish is in excellent condition with only a few small chips evident on the upper right portion of the rim. The most notable design changes are the shape of the object and the colors. The form has changed from standard plates and bowls to a deep basin (see "fig. 29" for a side view). Distinct from prior works examined, the color scheme used to decorate this dish includes: cool white, light cobalt blue, and deep reddish brown copper luster. Decorative elements include: (1) Floral and vegetative motifs; (2) Geometric motifs; (3) Figurative representation; and (4) Calligraphic inscription.

In the floral and vegetative motifs the bryony flower pattern has become subsumed in the background of larger leaf patterns resembling fern fronds—all depicted using the dark copper luster; light cobalt blue appears around the central calligraphic letters for parts of leaves and berry shapes and this color is used sparingly. The only

---

[275] Or, a width of almost 18 ½ inches and a depth of 5 ¼ inches.

Figure 28. *Deep Dish.* Manises, c.1440, width: 47.2 cm. The Cloisters Collection—Metropolitan Museum, New York City

Figure 29. *Deep Dish:* Side view

obvious geometric shapes are thin lines of light cobalt blue to delineated the inner side of the top rim and the inside rim of the bottom of the basin.

Figurative representation is inferred through a ring of seven crowns encircling the outer rim with each crown depicted in deep copper luster with a light cobalt blue outline. Wave shapes on the top of each crown rise in alternating leaf and ball shapes: on the left and ride are side views of three curling leaves and in the center a three-part leaf shape (similar to the top of a *fleur de lys* pattern) rises. Interspersed between the leaf clusters are two small spheres rising upon spikes.

At the center of the *Deep Dish* is what appears to be a calligraphic inscription. At first glance it looks like Gothic script—though only as three vertical lines, closely positioned so that their tops are touching, with one horizontal line running through the middle of the vertical lines.

Deductive Analysis

Becker explains that the Gothic script is indeed calligraphy—it is an interlocking Christian monogram 'IM.' 'I' and an 'M' are the first letters in Greek for 'Jesus Maria.'[276] The artisan has positioned the 'I' horizontally to cross through the 'M,' thus creating an equidistant cross and underscoring the Christian message at the center of the deep dish.

Speculative Analysis

These many changes in this object's form and decorative elements from prior objects examined suggest outside forces were influencing artisans causing innovations in design. A hint may be evident in the decorative elements on the exterior rim which

---

[276] Udo Becker, *Encyclopedia of Symbols*, 54.

features seven crowns. Husband infers that the crowns perhaps indicate "a royal commission, whose rendering shows considerable ingenuity. The underside of the crown spills over the brim onto the inside wall of the basin, creating a distinctly three-dimensional appearance."[277] Without further research, it is difficult to know whether these changes were initiated by a patron who commissioned this work or the artisans themselves.

Islamic and Jewish Motifs

While there are numerous examples of cross-fertilization of Muslim and Jewish imagery in architecturally settings, illustrations and calligraphy forms in manuscripts, and paintings, for the purposes of this dissertation, only one luster glazed ceramic piece emerged.

Figure 30. *Seder Plate from Pre-Expulsion Spain.*

Descriptive Analysis

Created circa 1480, this *Seder Plate from Pre-Expulsion Spain* measures 57 centimeters in width[278] and is on display at The Israel Museum in Jerusalem. The color scheme includes four hues: creamy white, cobalt blue, and two tones of luster, light gold and dark copper. Unlike most of the prior objects examined where creamy white glaze serves as the background color for many surfaces, the use of creamy white is minimal on this *Seder Plate*. Also, the cobalt blue is used not to articulate decorative vegetative elements but to create background bands of color. Decorative elements include: (1) Floral and vegetative motifs; (2) Geometric motifs; and (3) Calligraphic inscription.

---

[277] Husband, "Valencian Lusterware," 28.
[278] Or, a width of almost 22 ½ inches.

Figure 30. *Seder Plate from Pre-Expulsion Spain.* Probably Valencia, c. 1480, width: 57 cm. The Israel Museum, Jerusalem

A flower with eight petals outlined in cobalt blue emerges from the center of the dish. Another thin band of cobalt blue filled with small white petals in circular patterns is delineated from the central flower by a white circle. Other floral and vegetative motifs are evident only on the outer rim of the plate. Curving flower petal shapes, arranged diagonally and symmetrically, fill the plate's outer rim. Within the forty five petal shapes, fifteen of them contain small rendering of flowers and leaves; the other petal shapes are filled with geometrical patterns such as circles, cross-hatched lines, and diamond shapes.

Geometric motifs include outlined circles and five bands of decoration. The inner rim is marked by three concentric circles—a center thin blue circle framed by two outer white circles. Moving inward, filling the inner edge of the bowl is a series of light gold rectangles lined up diagonally appearing like leaning dominoes. Two thin circles of white and deep copper outline the next decorative band of dynamically linked triangles, diamond, and arch shapes. Within each of the diamond shapes are more diamonds and "x" shapes and within the arches are clusters of evenly spaced fine lines radiating perpendicular from the next cobalt blue band. Moving inward, the cobalt blue band is decorated simple with repeated clusters of four small almost crossed white lines—though the center is left blue.

All of these dynamic floral, vegetative, and geometric motifs serve to frame the focal point of the *Seder Plate*: the Hebrew calligraphy inscribed in dark copper luster rests on a band of light gold.

Deductive Analysis

The Hebrew calligraphy, as explained by Raccah-Djivre, describes the components of the Passover festival: *pesach* (Pachal lamb), *matzah* (unleavened bread), *maror* (bitter herbs), and *seder* (the ritual meal commemorating Passover).[279] The Passover service, according to Victoria and Albert Museum curatorial notes, "sets out in

---

[279] Daisy Raccah-Djivre, *The Jewish World: 365 Days, from the Collections of the Israel Museum, Jerusalem* (New York: Harry N. Abrams, 2004), 213.

order the events in the book of Exodus when the Jewish people were liberated from slavery and left Egypt."[280]

Raccah-Djivre attributes the origin stating, "[t]he plate was probably produced by Valencia potters."[281] While this plate is unique, it does bear some similarities to previous luster glaze ceramic wares examined. The color palette with the combination of cobalt blue and dark copper luster glaze is similar to the *Deep Dish* in Figure 28. In addition, the curved petal shapes on the outer rim may be mimicking metalwork patterns recalling the composition of the *Brasero Dish* in Figure 23. Visible at the top edge of the rim is one singular hole bored through the clay (instead of the two holes which pierce the rims of many other plates) which suggests this piece was intended to be on display when not in use.

This luster ware object was not only intended for display but also for use during the rituals of a Passover Seder meal. As a ritual object, this luster glazed *Seder Plate* is unique even in a collection of other Jewish ritual objects as explained by Daisy Raccah-Djivre, Chief Curator of the Department of Judiaca at the Israel Museum: "This plate, the earliest known Seder plate in existence, belongs to a small group of Jewish ceremonial objects that survived the expulsion from Spain."[282]

Speculative Analysis

This plate is the largest of all examples of a luster glazed ceramic ware examined in this dissertation as it measures 57 centimeters in width. The only other example close is the *Bowl* decorated with a ship in figure 9 made in Málaga measuring 51.2 centimeters

---

[280] "Seder Plate: Note," Victoria and Albert Museum, accessed February 7, 2016, http://collections.vam.ac.uk/item/O72144/seder-plate-yitzak-lieb-bar/.
[281] Daisy Raccah-Djivre, "New: Passover Plate," *The Israel Museum Newsletter* (2014), accessed August 18, 2016, http://www.english.imjnet.org.il/article_302.
[282] Raccah-Djivre, *The Jewish World,* 211.

in width. The size suggests possible ritual use according to Raccah-Djivre; she states that "given its comparatively large size, may have been used in a pre-Passover synagogue ritual."[283]

The execution of the Hebrew calligraphy contains spelling errors and raises questions. Outlines of the Hebrew letters are evident upon close examination suggesting care and perhaps unfamiliarity with the script Raccah-Djivre suggests: "Although the plate's decorator outlined the letters before completing it, it is probable that the wording was not thoroughly checked, as there are spelling errors (in the words *matzah* and *pesah)*, and some letters are improperly formed. This may indicate that a Jew commissioned the plate from a non-Jewish craftsman who was unfamiliar with the Hebrew characters." [284] However, Rabbinical student Lee Bearson disagrees with this conclusion stating that while there are three spelling errors, "most of the replacement letters sound the same as the proper letters, it seems that the person who wrote this could read Hebrew… someone who knows Hebrew, but not well."[285]

While it is assumed that the person who commissioned this *Seder Plate* was Jewish, the faith of the artisan who created it is unknown. Robin Cembalast, Executive Editor of ARTnews, notes that there are many examples of Iberian Jews working side-by-side with Christian artisans in a Catholic altarpiece.[286] Cembalest suggests that in addition to Jewish craftsmen found to be "executing objects of the most sacred nature such as crucifixes for church use" there were cases of "Christian craftsmen producing

---

[283] Raccah-Djivre, "Passover Plate."
[284] Raccah-Djivre, *The Jewish World*, 213.
[285] The errors: "*Matzah* is spelled with the letter *ayin* rather than a *hey*; *seder* is spelled with a *vav* rather than a *dalet*; *pesach* is spelled with a *chaf* rather than a *chet*." Lee Bearson, e-mail message to author, December 11, 2015.
[286] Cembalest, "Torah in the Altarpiece."

some of the commonplace ritual objects required by the Jewish community."[287] Further studies may uncover further information about the artisans and their religious affiliations working in the pottery studios in Valencia.

Conclusions

Valencia, a city in the Kingdom of Aragon, which returned to Christian rule in 1238 became an environment of religious tolerance based on the system used by Islamic Iberian rulers. Since religious wars between Christians and Muslims had subsided, Valencia cultivated not only toleration but peace which allowed for creative and cultural exchanges.

Production of luster ware ceramics in Valencia was enhanced due to (1) Geographic proximity to lucrative trade routes; (2) Excellent and abundant sources of clay on from the Turia river banks; and (3) An abundant supply of skilled artisans who had migrated from Málaga. At first, pottery producers in Valencia did not try to distinguish their work from the traditional Islamic decorative motifs and designs of luster glazed ceramics from Málaga. With increased prestige came increased commissions. Muslim and Múdejar artisans (along with the possibly Mozarab, Christian, and Jewish artisans) helped to create innovations in decorative motifs.

Valencia by the fifteenth century became the largest production center of luster glazed ceramics in Iberia, eventually surpassing the legacy of Málaga. Valencian luster wares became so renowned that ceramicists were commissioned by nobility and royaly throughout Europe and even for the Pope. Other artisans held luster glazed in such esteem that they replicated them in their paintings including a fifteenth century painting

---

[287] Cembalest, "Torah in the Altarpiece."

of The Last Supper from northern Spain which replicates a set of Valencian "*Ave Maria*" luster ware on the table in front of Jesus.

Valencian artisans created numerous examples of luster glazed ceramics with Christian family coats of arms using some of the traditional Islamic decorative motifs to offset the coats of arms. In combining Islamic and Christian Motifs, artisans featured Christian motifs in the center and used outer rims to feature combinations of Gothic calligraphic messages embellished with Islamic decorative motifs. In the final example, a monumental *Seder Plate* combines Islamic and Jewish motifs and features a central design of Hebrew calligraphy. As with several of the luster glazed ceramics with Christian messages inscribed in Gothic style Latin calligraphy, the occasion of spelling errors brings into focus the question of who was transcribing the message. Further research could shed light on many questions regarding the complex mix of cultural and religious identities of the artisans working together at a unique moment of history.

Chapter Four
Conclusion

The nearly eight hundred years of Islamic rule in Iberia left lasting visual, cultural, and religious imprints on the entire Iberian Peninsula, as well as throughout Europe and the Mediterranean regions. In the final embattled two hundred years of Islamic rule on a much diminished sliver of the Iberian Peninsula, Muslim artisans produced a new style of pottery in both Islamic ruled and Christian ruled territories. Using metallic glazing techniques brought by Muslim artisans from Egypt and Persia, artisans in Iberia created dazzling reflective luster glazed ceramics. The mix of Muslim, Christian and Jewish faith traditions within Iberia led to a mix of religious motifs being inscribed upon multiple forms of luster ware.

Key to this investigation has been the question of how were these different types of religious motifs used in Málaga and Valencia to decorate luster glazed ceramics? Did the religious motifs stay separate? Did they blend into a new hybrid symbolism, or did they combine while staying distinct? While contemplating any conclusions, it is important to remember that any analysis of luster glazed ceramics from this era is based upon a limited pool of surviving artifacts due to the many intensive battles and wars in the Málaga region. Given this caveat and given the geographical and socio-political contexts, some conclusions about the ways artisans and patrons in late Medieval Iberia understood the use of multiple religious motifs on luster glazed ceramics begin to emerge.

Why Málaga Excelled Initially

In examining the simultaneous evolution of luster glazed ceramic production in Málaga and Valencia, Málaga ascended to prominence first due to the number of skilled artisans and due to the royal patronage. Muslim artisans fleeing political upheaval from other Islamic ruled regions such as Egypt and Persia would have migrated first to the Iberian area under Nasrid rule (as opposed to the Christian ruled territories of Iberia). While Málaga became renowned for its exported luster ware, it also served as the premier production center for Nasrid Dynasty rulers who commissioned luster glazed ceramics for the Alhambra Palace—specifically, the monumental body of works now called the Alhambra Vases.

The three Alhambra Vases investigated in this dissertation display traditional Islamic motifs combining: (1) Floral and vegetative imagery, (2) Geometric symbols, and (3) Calligraphic inscriptions. The different styles of symbolism and Arabic calligraphy on each of the vases evoke different elements of Islam as it would relate to the contemporary Muslim viewers in *Al-Andalus*. The messages inscribed in each vase range from equating the kingship of the Nasrid rulers to the Divine power of *Allah*, to 'sacred hand' imagery which suggests a correlation between *Allah*'s power and the King's power, to, finally, a poem that invites the "onlooker" into personal contemplation of divine presence in earthly beauty. These motifs are used in ways that remain within the sphere of traditional Islamic imagery.

The next two dishes from Málaga use decorative schemes combining some traditional Islamic motifs (such as (1) Floral and vegetative imagery, (2) Geometric symbols, and (3) Figurative representations) with Christian motifs. Of note, in the two dishes examined, the distinction of what is Islamic and what is Christian is ambiguous. For example, the first dish may or may not display a Christian image: it shows a figure on horseback about to spear a giant serpent. As such, it has been assumed to be a Christian image of St. George and the Dragon. However, since both Muslims and Christians revere St. George, this could be an Islamic homage.

The second dish depicts a specific kind of Portuguese ship. Though there is a tradition in Islamic ceramics of depicting ships, this ship notably displays a cross on its main sail. The deduction that this is an image of a Christian ship, most likely commissioned by a Christian Portuguese mariner, is underscored when considering the prominent inclusion of fish, an early symbol denoting Christians, upon which the ship appears to rest.

Thus, while Málaga produced a large body of luster glazed ceramic works with solely traditional Islamic motifs, Málagan artisans also produced luster glazed ceramic works with an apparent combination of Islamic and Christian motifs—though the interpretation of how these motifs are combined, whether based on an artisan's or patron's motivation is not definitively clear.

How Different Styles Emerge in Valencia

While Valencia was a part of the Christian ruled Kingdom of Aragon, by the mid-thirteenth century its Christian King established an environment of religious tolerance based on the system used by earlier Islamic Iberian rulers. Given this new environment of religious tolerance and political stability in Valencia, in ensuing years, as strife and warfare increased in Málaga, many Muslim artisans migrated to Valencia. This influx of Muslim artisans to Valencia in the thirteenth and fourteenth century led to the development of multiple styles of luster glazed ceramics. As the peace was lasting in Valencia, Muslim, *Múdejar*, *Mozarab*, Christian, and Jewish artisans could flourish without the constant threat of destruction. Artisans from Valencia decorated luster ware with the following combinations of religious images: (1) Traditional Islamic motifs, (2) Islamic motifs and Christian Coats of Arms, (3) Islamic motifs and Christian messages, and, in one known example, (3) Islamic motifs and Jewish messages.

The first four dishes investigated in this dissertation which were produced in Valencia contain traditional Islamic motifs including (1) Floral and vegetative imagery, (2) Geometric symbols, and (3) Calligraphic inscriptions. The bowl with a sacred hand on a lustrous gold surface (*Bowl with Fatima's Hand*) in figure 13, bears striking contrast to the sacred hands depicted on the monumental *Alhambra Vase (2)* in figure 3 from Málaga. The most notable difference is their size. While the Alhambra Vase is nearly as tall as a human, the bowl from Valencia could be cupped within one's hands. The intimacy of this object (made in Christian dominated territory) underscores that it was not meant for a public palatial setting but perhaps within a more private home setting.

The next three Valencian-made dishes show how artisans tried to imitate the imagery used in Málaga: these dishes at first glance stick closely to the traditional Islamic decorative schemes. Upon inspection, the final example, the *Plate* in figure 16 deviates in its traditional decorative scheme as it combines four palm trees and four strips of pseudo *Kufic* Arabic script in what could be seen as two intersecting equidistant crosses. The inclusion of pseudo *Kufic* script alone demonstrates a diminishment of Islamic influence as it is a script intended to replicate Arabic *Kufic* script but is not actually legible or meaningful. The combination of equidistant cross shapes may show the subtle Christian influence or may be an intentional blending of traditions.

In the remaining examples of Valencian-made luster glazed ceramics investigated that combine Islamic and Christian or Jewish motifs, the Islamic motifs serve as an outside border framing a central Christian or Jewish motif. It is as if the Islamic elements fade into the background. Thus the central Christian messages or one Jewish message become the foreground and the Islamic images the background in most of the Valencian dishes. Notably, in three subsequently examined objects, the *Dish* in figure 19, the *Plate* in figure 24, and the *Deep Dish* in figure 28, even the border becomes inscribed with Christian motifs. The seven crowns on the bordering rim of figure 28 may be a visual show of force of Christian re-established dominion, perhaps the seven Christian Kingdoms of Iberia. The inclusion of Gothic style calligraphic script, in Catalan ("fig. 19") or in Latin ("fig. 24"), enhances and underscores the explicit central Christian image on each dish.

Of note, the calligraphic inscriptions on Valencian-made luster glazed ceramics often included errors. The potential mix of Muslim, *Múdejar*, *Mozarab*, Christian, and Jewish artisans may explain some of the mistakes or spelling errors whether they are in the rendering of *Kufic* ("fig. 16"), Catalan ("fig. 19"), Latin ("fig. 24"), or Hebrew ("fig. 30"). The occasion of these inscribed spelling errors brings into focus the question of who was transcribing the messages—a question with no clear cut answer.

Why Valencia surpassed Málaga

Though the quantity and quality of works initially differed, by the fifteenth century, Valencia surpassed Málaga in quantity, variety, and quality of luster glazed

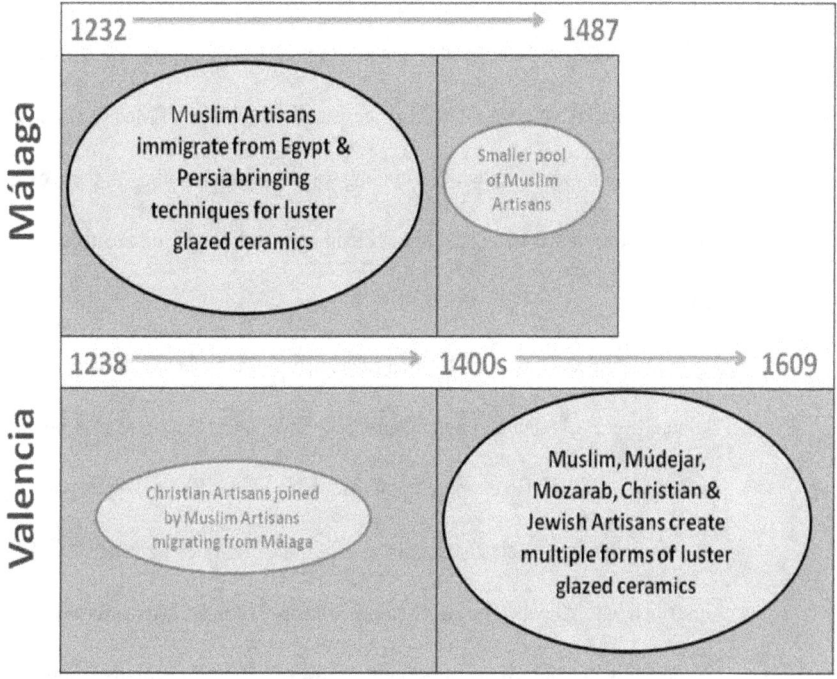

Table 4. *Luster Glazed Ceramics in Iberia: Malaga & Valencia*

ceramic ware produced. The primary reason for Valencia's success was due to the Christian re-conquest and establishment of peace—its land was no longer under siege. In contrast, Málaga and its environs the Kingdom of Granada, were under an almost constant state of siege during the thirteenth through fifteenth centuries.

Final Refelctions

The luster glazed ceramics of Málaga and Valencia were created within two very different dynamic environments. In each context, Islamic, Christian, and Jewish cultures interacted—but with very different power dynamics. Thus the works created in each location reflect different ways of combining religious motifs.

In Málaga, where Islamic rulers were trying to hold on to political power, Islamic decorative motifs took precedence over other modes. For example, the monumental Alhambra Vases reflect clear Islamic messages of a strong allegiance between divine dominion and the Nasrid rulers. In other smaller examples of Málaga luster ware, Islamic motifs remain prominent while including some Christian motifs. In these examples, the two religious motifs co-exist without blending—each retains distinguishable characteristics.

In Valencia, where Christian rulers had re-established their hold after five hundred years of Islamic reign, Islamic decorative motifs began to incorporate Christian and Jewish motifs. Here too, religious motifs co-exist without blending and with each retaining distinguishable characteristics. The one example of a luster ware Seder Plate inscribed with a Jewish message reflects a balance of Islamic decorative elements combined with the Hebrew inscription. However, Islamic decorative motifs lose their prominence in Valencian luster ware when combined with Christian motifs. Instead of being at the core of the decorative schemes, Islamic motifs are no longer connected to Arabic calligraphy; what pseudo *Kufic* script is used becomes illegible and is used as a pattern. In contrast, the Christian motifs begin to take precedence. Christian symbolism varies from implicit, in the exposition of Christian family coats of arms, to explicit, in the Gothic style calligraphic messages.

Thus, while Islamic, Christian, and Jewish motifs were combined on luster glazed ceramics in late Medieval Iberia in both Málaga and Valencia, these motifs did not blend into a new hybrid art form: they remained distinct and distinguishable. The images do not fuse—they are used various combinations side by side. This juxtaposition of imagery raises a question of visual literacy, that is, the extent to which artisans and patrons understood the decorative motifs of each other's faith traditions.

Specific areas for further inquiry include: (1) Searching in private collections and among the broken shards in museums for clues to determine the extent to which luster glazed ceramics combined Islamic and Jewish motifs; (2) Comparative studies of calligraphic inscriptions on luster glazed ceramics to determine patterns in linguistic slips, errors, and misspellings with the hopes of potentially identifying the religious backgrounds of artisans; and (3) Researching documents in which patrons order luster glazed ceramics to determine how specific their requests were regarding decorative motifs. With this further research a more nuanced understanding can emerge of how Islamic, Christian, and Jewish artisans and patrons negotiated the decorative motifs used on the luster glazed ceramics in late Medieval Iberia.

Postscript: The Decline of Luster Glazed Ceramics in Iberia

Suddenly, in the early sixteenth century, the luster glazed ceramics industry in Valencia began to decline even before the expulsions of Muslims from Spain in 1609. The withdrawal of noble and royal patronage by the middle of the fifteenth century, a major cause of this decline, may have been, in part, induced by the shortcomings of later craftsmen, but, more probably, by the development of the 'Renaissance taste,'[288] that is, the preference for Italian ceramic ware known as *majolica*.[289] The decline of Valencian luster glazed ceramics was gradual and determined by changing tastes of those commissioning the work.

The demise of Málaga, on the other hand, was more abrupt and brutal. In 1487, Spanish Catholic forces laid siege to Málaga and re-conquered the port city enslaving those residents who were not slaughtered. By 1492, Catholic forces regained the capitol Granada thus putting an end to Islamic rule in Iberia. As of today, there is a National Museum of Ceramics in Valencia with a significant collection of lusterware and a small Ceramics Museum in Málaga with mostly broken shards. Due to this series of events and the succeeding waves of expulsions of Muslims and Jews from Spain, there are perhaps more surviving intact works of fourteenth and fifteenth century era luster glazed ceramics from the Iberian Peninsula preserved in collections and museums throughout the world than in Spain.

---

[288] Italian Renaissance paintings influenced the decorative schemes of ceramic ware such that they "depicted historical or mythical scenes." Husband, "Valencian Lusterware," 19.

[289] The term *majolica* (also called *mailocia*) is believed to be derived from the island of Majorca, an island due east of Valencia which was "a major point of distribution for Iberian luster glazed ceramics as they were exported throughout the Mediterranean." Caiger-Smith, *Lustre Pottery,* 113.

Appendix 1. GLOSSARY

Al-Andalus	(Arabic) The southern region of the Iberian peninsula when under Islamic rule; the region known in English as 'Andalusia.'
Converso	Jews who converted to Christianity.
Hamsa	*Hamsa* means five in Arabic. This symbol of a raised hand with closed fingers has multiple associations with many Mediterranean cultures. Within Muslim cultures it is also referred to as the *'Hand of Fatima,'* Levantine Christians call it the *'Hand of Mary'* and within Sephardic and Mizrahi Jewish cultures it is associated with the Hebrew letter *Shin*, the first letter of *Shaddai*—one of the names of God.
Khamsa	Romanized spelling of *hamsa*.
Loza dorada	(Spanish) Golden luster glazed lusterware ceramics.
Mizrahi	Jews who never left the Middle East.
Moor or Morrish	Moor means 'dark' has been used to describe Muslims who arrived and settled the Iberian Peninsula. It "has acquired…a racial veneer" and is seen by Muslims as a pejorative term referring to the people who came from Morocco: "The Spanish equivalent *moro*….can [be] used to designate, sometimes pejoratively, and almost appropriate vagueness, that 'other' that was not Christian or Jewish."[290] Muslims themselves, however, did not use the term to refer to themselves.
Moriscos	Muslims who converted to Christianity.
Mozarab	'Arabized' Christians who adopted Muslim customs such as types of clothing and food and speaking Arabic.
Mudejar	Muslims who converted to Christianity.
Muwalladūn	Christian natives of Spain whose ancestors converted to Islam.
Sephardic	Jews from the Iberian Peninsula.
Taifa	In Arabic *taifa* means 'party' or 'faction;' in Islamic Iberia it meant regions that splintered or broke away into separate *Taifa* Kingdoms.

---

[290] Menocal, "Visions," 12.

Umayyad	The *Umayyad* Dynasty was the second of the four major Arab caliphates established after the death of Muhammad. The *Umayyad* Dynasty in Syria ruled from their capital Damascus from 661until 750. The Umayyad Caliphate in Iberia ruled from their capital Córdoba from 756-1031.

Appendix 2. CERAMICS DEFINITIONS

Absorbency	The ability of clay to soak up water.
Bisque fire	A first lower temperature firing to make pots less fragile for glazing.
Bone dry	Unfired clay from which water has evaporated; it only contains the amount of moisture in atmosphere.
Ceramic	A clay object made into a permanent shape by firing in a kiln.
Clay	A moist earth of decomposed rock used in products such as pottery, bricks, tiles, and sculpture.
Clay body	A mixture of two or more clays to obtain a desired color, plasticity, strength, or fired density.
Firing	Heating ceramic clays and glazes in a kiln to maturity.
Glaze	A vitreous coating which fuses to the surface of a clay body during firing in order to prevent the penetration of liquids. It presents a decorative surface which is easily cleaned. Glazes can be shiny or matte.
Greenware	Unfired, but dried clay pieces.
Kiln	A special furnace that reaches high temperatures for firing clay products.
Leather hard	The damp but stiffened stage in drying clay. Puncturing holes, adding handles or other additions can be made at this point.
Nonfunctional	Created mainly for decoration rather than practical use.
Plasticity	The quality of clay which allows it to be manipulated, shaped or molded without cracking or crumbling; workability.
Sgraffito	Scratching designs on pottery.
Slip	Clay diluted with water to the consistency of cream, used for shaping and joining pieces of clay.

Throwing	Creating vessels on a potter's wheel.
Underglaze	Colors that can be painted on greenware or bisque that will show through a clear overglaze.
Viscosity	The relative runniness of a glaze.
Vitrify	To harden; turn to stone. A glassy, non-porous state caused by heat or fusion.
Wedging	Kneading moist clay to force air bubbles out and wet clay particles to form a good working texture.
Wheel	For making pots; driven by hand or foot.

Appendix 3. ALHAMBRA VASES

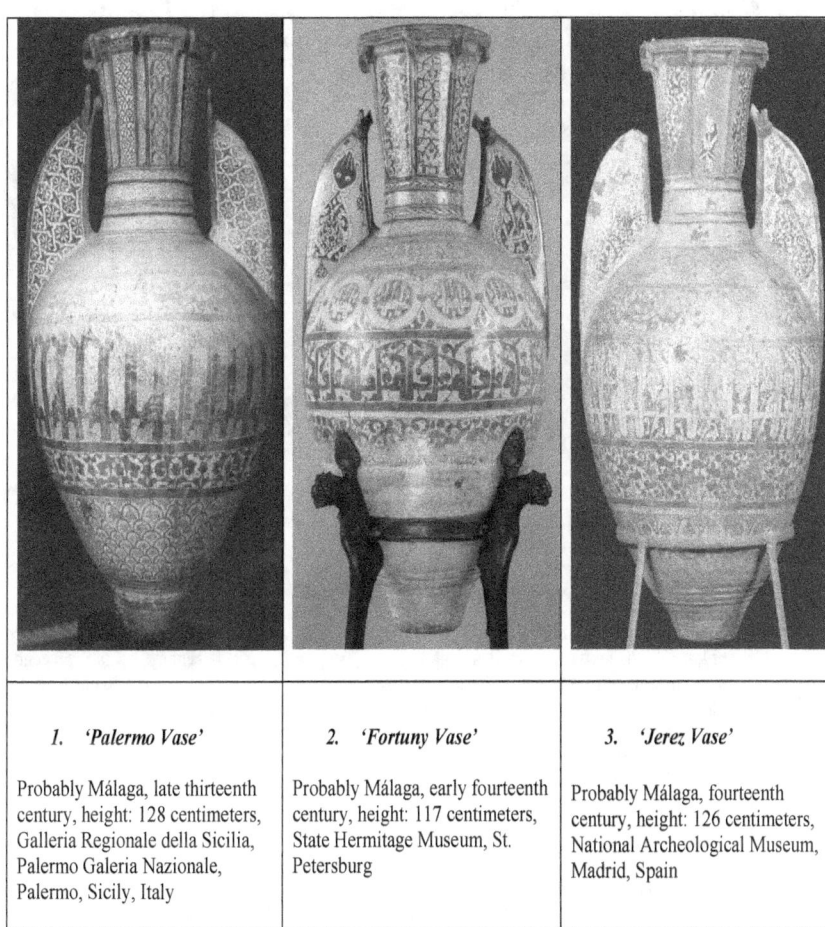

1. *'Palermo Vase'*	2. *'Fortuny Vase'*	3. *'Jerez Vase'*
Probably Málaga, late thirteenth century, height: 128 centimeters, Galleria Regionale della Sicilia, Palermo Galeria Nazionale, Palermo, Sicily, Italy	Probably Málaga, early fourteenth century, height: 117 centimeters, State Hermitage Museum, St. Petersburg	Probably Málaga, fourteenth century, height: 126 centimeters, National Archeological Museum, Madrid, Spain

4. 'Osma Vase' Probably Málaga, fourteenth century, height: unknown, Valencia Institute of Don Juan, Madrid, Spain	*5. 'Simonetti Vase'* Probably Málaga, c. 1300-1350, height: unknown, Museum of the Alhambra, Granada, Spain	*6. Untitled Vase* Probably Málaga, fourteenth century, height: 150 centimeters, Nationalmuseum, Stockholm, Sweden

7. 'Freer Vase' Probably Málaga, late fourteenth-early fifteenth century, height: 77.2 centimeters, Smithsonian Institution: Freer Gallery, Washington, D.C.	**8. 'Antelope Vase'** Probably Málaga, fourteenth or fifteenth century, height: 135 centimeters, Museum of the Alhambra, Granada	**9. 'Hornos Vase'** Probably Málaga, c. 1351-1375, height: 134 centimeters National Archeological Museum, Madrid, Spain
NO IMAGE AVAILABLE		
10. 'Heilbronner Vase' Formerly in Germany, the *'Heilbronner Vase'* was sold to a Spaniard in the J. Seligmann sale in 1925; in 1936 it was destroyed in a fire in a customs house. No photographic record was found by this author.		

www.ingramcontent.com/pod-product-compliance
Lightning Source LLC
Chambersburg PA
CBHW051439290426
44109CB00016B/1613